T0375205

My Life

CAROLYN PETERSEN

authorHOUSE®

AuthorHouse™
1663 Liberty Drive
Bloomington, IN 47403
www.authorhouse.com
Phone: 1 (800) 839-8640

Published by AuthorHouse 08/03/2018

ISBN: 978-1-5462-5375-4 (sc)
ISBN: 978-1-5462-5373-0 (hc)
ISBN: 978-1-5462-5374-7 (e)

Contents

My Life

This book is written for and dedicated to my Daughter, Gena. There will be information in this book that has never been revealed, and is only being revealed now to give her a better understanding of how things have turned out in my life, and how you can always make it through bad times if you lean on God and have the love of family and friends. I hope she will not take this information the wrong way and think I am belittling her Dad in any way because that is not my intent. I loved J.D. with all my heart and soul just as much the day he passed away as the day I married him. He was a good man inside and out and was always willing to help anyone that needed help. He was a good Christian man and loved his family more than life. That being said, we all have our faults, me included, and none of us are perfect. If we were, we would not be walking on this earth.

Chapter 1

On June 4, 1944, my mother was enjoying the day at Bethel Memorial Day with my Aunt Eunice when she had to be rushed to the Winnsboro Hospital where I was delivered by Dr. Stuart, who was a D.O. in Winnsboro. I weighed in at less than 6 pounds and weighed this until I was almost 6 weeks old at which time my mother and daddy and Aunt Myrtie started bringing me to a specialist in Dallas, Texas to see why I wasn't gaining weight. I guess it was because they could not find a formula that I could keep down. I would like to find the specialist that got me started eating and gaining weight because he has caused me a lot of misery in my life with weight problems. Ha!!!

Anyhow, he got me started gaining weight and I was soon so big that my mother couldn't carry me around and had to pull me around in a red wagon wherever we went. I guess they did not have the money to buy a stroller. And, of course, I had a big sister that was very petite and very feisty. However, she caused mother and daddy a lot more trouble than their little fat baby.

I do not remember too much about my childhood until I started walking and talking and then I was a real pistol because I repeated everything that Mother and Daddy said in front of me. I stayed in trouble because of my mouth. I was raised by a daddy who knew no fear and his theory was that if you want your daughters to mind, don't tell them to do anything they do not want to do, and a mother who feared everything. This was because she had witnessed my two-year-old sister, Joye Anne being run over on her tricycle by their next door neighbor. I think my mother was just lucky to survive this. However, she did have a breakdown that affected her nerves for the rest of her life.

I was raised in a little white house on the hill. This was a small house with two bedrooms, a living room, a small bathroom with a shower that I was not allowed to use except to hide in, and a pretty large kitchen with a table in it. We had a detached garage with the wringer washing machine and rinse tubs and a storeroom that later became my sister's school room that I was only allowed into if I wanted to play school and let her teach me, which, of course, was never. I was into playing and not learning. I could go in if she was gone and be my own teacher or play dolls. I'm sure if she had had a key I wouldn't have gotten into it then. Mother would bring in the No. 2 washtub and fill it with water for our baths. Of course I was always the last to have a bath because I was always the dirtiest, I guess. I can remember Mother always raised her legs and washed her feet in the lavatory and I thought that looked so good that I would try it.

I got my tiny little red chair and stood on it and tried to throw my leg up into the sink and, of course, the chair tipped over and I hit my head on the gas outlet and then was in trouble once again. I remember the kitchen had high cabinets that I could hardly reach, and that is where I had to have my hair washed in the sink and always rinsed with vinegar water. I had long hair and always dreaded hair washing day.

If this little white house could talk, it could tell many stories about our family, and especially me. My sister, who I always called "Nannie," which she hated, but Mother said I could not say Sandy, so it was always "Nannie," and I shared a small bedroom on the back of the house that was very cold in the winter. We slept in the same bed with an imaginary line down the middle. I wasn't allowed to get one toe across that imaginary line or I was in big trouble. At some point in time an extra room was added to the east side of the house and that room doubled as a bedroom and mother's sewing room. I think they added that for an extra bedroom in case we had overnight company. It was really a nice room and we all loved it.

We had a very large squirrel cage in the back yard and had supposedly pet squirrels. This was a joke because they were really pretty wild. We also had a chicken pen and a chicken coop where the hens laid eggs that we had to gather and eat. We had cows down at the barn, which I would later have to help milk, but I can't remember how old I was when I started milking the cows. We also had an occasional bull named Bimbo that I never could understand why he just came to stay for a short visit. I think I was told that we were keeping him for someone. This was rather confusing because I knew nothing about the birds and bees, but was told that the cows went down in the trees in the pasture and found their calves and then brought them to the barn, or we would have to go down in the pasture and find them. I was raised thinking that calves were just found down in the pasture. I am sure my sister knew better but never told me. She wasn't nearly as naïve as I was.

Actually, we didn't have to milk the cows because we had a milking machine. We would just wash their teats and put the milking machine on them and then take it off and strip the milk from them; I guess because the milking machine could not get it all. I would hang my milk pail on the handle bars of our little red bicycle and fly down to the barn to help milk.

I remember how I hated to milk the cows during fly season because they would continuously swish their tail in your face and if they had bowel trouble, the tail was not always too clean. Also, you would have a quarter of a pail to a half a pail of milk and they would decide to hit a fly with their leg and would step in the pail and splash milk all in your face. It was not only a nuisance, but it wasted the milk because you then had to pour it into the kitten bowl or pour it out. I hated this because we used this milk to strain, bottle and deliver to the neighbors. Another job of my mother. I guess they paid her a little bit and we needed the money, so she would do it. I'm sure she didn't make much, but in those days every little bit helped.

The good part about selling milk to the neighbors was that I got to go with Mother to deliver it. After delivering milk, we would always stop back in at Dal Hagan's grocery store and get a Dr. Pepper. He would always give me a piece of candy or gum, and this made the milking and all of the work worthwhile for me.

I had more pinches from Mother in this little store than you could ever imagine. To begin with, the store usually had men in it, and then there was me and Mother. This is the little store where I couldn't understand why we always had to buy just plain napkins, which was not often because we usually used a cup towel and passed it around the table when we had a meal. We called it the "rag." I begged Mother to please buy some sanitary napkins instead of plain napkins because we had never had any of those. Of course the store was full of men, so I was quickly yanked out of there. This is also the store where I told Dal that I had tasted everything in that store except (and I looked all around and spotted a box of Kotex) those

Kotex up there. Once again; a quick exit for me and Mother. Of course, nobody ever told me what I had said wrong, so it was hard for me to understand what was going on.

Often when we made the milk delivery, I would get to stay at Dina's house, and was very happy about it. She had the best things to play with and we always had a good time together. She had dolls (with clothes) and her favorite doll was named Laureen. Rightfully so, because she adored her mother. This doll had so many clothes that Mrs. Dodgen had made for her. and had an outfit just like Dina's because she would make Dina's clothes and make an outfit for her doll out of the scraps. Her mother would make us a pallet on the floor and we would play dolls for hours. She would even chip a bowl of ice and give us on a hot day. Of course, I loved playing with her dolls with all of the clothes because I had to pin rags on my dolls for clothes and they didn't have very many rag clothes. Dina also had a porch swing in her front yard that we always loved to swing on. She also had a limb on a tree out back that made a perfect horse. We were really into being cowgirls, especially her, and loved riding that horse. I think its name was "Trigger." However, one day I stayed with her and realizing after Mother left that I would miss my Dr. Pepper, I started crying and wanting to go home. It was all about the Dr. Pepper, but I told Mrs. Dodgen that I was sick and wanted to go home. Of course she did not have a car and could not take me and we had no phones to call my mother to come and get me. I think she ended up walking me home because I would not quit crying, and, of course, by then it was too late for the Dr. Pepper, so the only thing I got out of that was into trouble with my mother. This also kept me from being able to stay at Dina's for the day for quite some time.

We had pigs which I loved until they became big hogs and then they were not very friendly. We had a hay loft in the barn that we could climb up into and play. I loved going up the ladder into the loft but hated coming down.

Mother also had a beautiful rose garden that she loved, but I didn't like very much because it required work, which interrupted with my playing. We had to pull weeds and hoe this rose garden and it was hard for me to understand the purpose of it. Of course Mother loved it and I guess it was a pleasure for her to work in it. I don't think she had too many pleasures because she had to cook, clean, wash and iron, make all of our clothes and then cut the grass. Needless to say, she didn't have a washer and dryer and dishwasher either. Also, she had to use a push mower to mow the acre we lived on. I think Daddy helped her occasionally, but I mostly remember her doing it. And you know, I never heard her complain about all of this work.

We also had a grape vineyard where we raised grapes for jelly, which Mother made. And the dreaded storm cellar behind the vineyard. The storm cellar was my most unfavorite place to go because it seemed that storms always came in the middle of the night and I hated hearing Mother say, "Get up girls and get your clothes on because it's coming up a cloud and we have to go to the cellar." This often meant running in the rain to get there in the middle of the night with a flashlight. We were usually the first ones there and had to go in with a flashlight and light the coal oil lantern. We would just get settled in with my little bed made out of a damp quilt when here would come all the neighbors; the Cottons across the road and the Shirleys from behind. This meant I had to give up my bench bed on the damp musty quilt so they would have a place to sit. I was always so happy when Ruben Shirley or Mother would raise the door of the cellar and look out and say, "I guess the storm has past, so we can go back to the house." Those were such good sounding words because I could now go back to bed.

We had our own private swimming hole down in the trees at the back of the pasture, which is also where our cows went to find baby calves (as I was told). This swimming hole always had very cool water because it was located back in the trees and was fed by a spring. This is where I learned to swim. It even had vines that we could swing out over the water and let go and fall in, if we were brave enough. I was sort of afraid of the water because I didn't know how to swim. However, my daddy took care of that when one day he just picked me up and pitched me in and told me to swim. It was either swim or drown because it was too deep to touch the bottom. I'm sure he would have saved me, but he just wanted to test what he had been trying to teach me; and I did it. Of course, he made a big deal out of how proud he was of me. We didn't have swimsuits and just went swimming in our shorts and tops. I guess Mother didn't know how to make swimsuits or didn't want to because she hated for us to go swimming because it was way too dangerous if you didn't know how to swim, and also she had a great fear of a body of water.

I always loved going to bed because I played hard all day long and when it was sundown, it was time for me to go to bed; no matter where we were or who was at our house. As I mentioned earlier, Mother and Daddy were quite social. They belonged to a square dance club and had square dances way too often for me because these interfered with my bedtime. We also went to singing conventions where Mother says was the only time my daddy ever spanked me. She said we had just gotten there and I started crying because I wanted to go home and go to bed. Oh well, anyhow I don't remember it, so that doesn't count. They played 42 quite often with the Coes and thank goodness, this was usually at our house. Sometimes I would stay up long enough to pop some popcorn for them and then off to bed I went. I just felt it was my job to pop the popcorn because they always told me it was just right and what a good job I did. When we had to go to the Coes' house, I would just crawl up on the couch and go to sleep. I wasn't a lot of trouble after sundown, as you can see.

We lived in a great neighborhood and always had something going on with the neighbors. We had neighborhood stews and when it was time to kill hogs, had chitlin suppers. This was quite disgusting, but we didn't have to eat them. We always had other food for those who didn't like chitlins. We always had these at the Coes' house, and they were quite smelly. At least it was a good playtime because the Dodgens always came and I had Dina to play with.

That little white house on the hill would probably tell about the time that we had a new kitten and Mother told my sister and me that we could keep the kitten in the house if we could get rid of the fleas. That is when my sister came up with the idea that we could use Mother's vacuum cleaner and suck the fleas off the cat. She always came up with good ideas, but there was just one problem and that was that I hold the kitten while she sucked the fleas off; and when she told me to hold onto something, I knew no matter what I should not let go. Needless to say, that kitten did not like the vacuum cleaner and scratched and clawed me while I was hanging onto it. It finally escaped and became a flying kitten. He flew up the curtains across the ceiling of the living room and was like a wildcat. Of course I got into trouble for letting go of him. Ha!!! I promise you that I did not let go, but the cat actually escaped. That's my story and I'm sticking to it.

I can remember playing paper dolls with my sister and when we were cutting them out, I told her to throw me the scissors and that is just what she did. The scissors hit me in the cheek just missing my eye, and once again, she was in trouble.

My daddy worked for Pat Campbell and sold John Deere tractors in Winnsboro and would have to go to Dallas to pick up parts. When Daddy went to Dallas, he would always bring my sister and me a six pack of beer. He didn't drink beer, but we loved it. This is a preface to my next story about getting into the refrigerator and drinking all the beer I wanted. Mother and Daddy could not figure out what was wrong with me because when I tried to get into the pickup I would just fall backwards laughing, of course, and then they sent me to the house and I tried to rock in the rocking chair and turned the rocking chair over. I finally broke down and told them I thought I just drank all of the beer that I could hold that was in the refrigerator. Everything was sooo funny and I'm sure they had trouble punishing me, but did make me stay at home since I could not get into the truck. I guess that was punishment enough because I loved to go.

Our little white house was near the railroad tracks and, therefore, we had a lot of hobos come to the house (always when Daddy was gone). My sister would grab her water gun and head for the shower that we were not allowed to use except for hiding in and Mother would grab me and we would hide behind the door where he was knocking. Of course I was nervous and every time he knocked I would giggle. My mother would cup her hand over my mouth to hold back my giggles, but they were still there. Eventually he would go on and we would come out of hiding.

This same train track had many bad wrecks with cars being hit by the train. It had no lights flashing or anything to warn people and they would just come over the hill and the train would be there and they would either hit it or the train would hit them. It was always very bad accidents. When we did have company for the night, which was not very often because we didn't have a place to put them, they would always say the train kept them awake. However, we never even heard it; I guess because we were so used to hearing it. If I was bored and didn't have anything else to do, I would just sit on the hill and count the train cars and then wave at the conductor in the caboose.

Our Christmases and birthdays were always special because we did not get gifts all year round. At Christmas, Daddy would always take us down in the pasture and we would cut our own Christmas tree and drag it to the house and then he would chop it off and put it on a stand. We would then decorate it. I was a big believer in Santa Claus, and still am. When my sister stopped believing in Santa Claus, I felt sorry for her because she did not get as much as I did for Christmas. I always told her she should just believe in Santa and she would get a lot more. Of course, the things that she was getting probably cost a lot more than what I was getting from Santa, but who cared because I just knew Santa brought mine. I remember one year she only got a Samsonite overnight bag and was so proud of it, but I got dolls and toys.

I always loved my birthday too and never let anybody forget it. I even posted signs around the house as reminders. These signs always said how many shopping days left until my birthday. And, of course, I always wanted a party. I know I had one party because we only have one picture of my birthday party. I'm sure that's because we didn't own a camera. My granddaddy had a Brownie and probably came to the party, or mother used it and took my picture. The nice part about not having a camera is that there are no pictures for me to think I was ugly in. Ha!!!

I always had long curls and hated them even though everybody would say how cute I was and how they loved my curls. Dal Hagan that owned the grocery store across the highway from us told me one day he would love to have one of my curls, and you can probably guess, I went home and got the scissors and cut him one. Oh boy, did I ever mess up with that one. Mother was so very upset with me, and, believe it or not, I hated making my mother or daddy unhappy.

As I said earlier, my mother and daddy were very social and had neighbors pop in in the evening, (a lot of times uninvited) to play 42. Sometimes mother would say that we could go to town or somewhere if Garlan and Lela Coe did not come to play 42. Of course, this is all I needed to hear and when I saw them drive up, as they did so often, I met them at the pickup and told them that mother said if they did not show up we could do something else, so I thought they should probably leave. Once again, just repeating what I had heard.

We also had a neighbor, Mrs. Elkins, who would come to our house almost every morning with her pack of cigarettes and sit at the kitchen table while mother tried to work, drinking coffee and smoking cigarettes. Mother said one time after she left that she wished she would quit coming every day and smoking those cigarettes and drinking coffee because she had work to do and could not get anything done. That's all I needed to hear and the next day when she came walking up, I met her and told her what mother had said. I'm sure it hurt her feelings, but mother smoothed it over and the visits did become less frequent.

We did not have company real often for dinner, but we had out-of-town guests just back from Saudi Arabia. This was a man and his family that Daddy worked with in the oilfield. Of course, I had to show off for them and was taken from the table to the bathroom by my daddy where I had to stay for the rest of the meal. Once again, it was my mouth. I thought I would surely die in the bathroom because I thought he locked me in, but eventually learned that he only closed the door. More than anything else, I was heartbroken because my daddy never punished me.

Growing up, I was so lucky because even though we lived about a mile and a half out of town, we had neighborhood kids to play with. Betty Turrentine lived just across the railroad tracks from us and her mother loved to visit with Mother so they would come and we would play. Dina lived just down the road and her parents and my parents were good friends, so I played with her a lot. I had a little, what I thought was rich girl, Winifred Robb ("Winnie") that lived in the brick house on the hill just up from us and we really liked each other a lot and played together real often. They were very different from our family. However, everybody liked my mother and daddy and her parents would let her play with me anytime. All we had to do was run up or down the hill and we were together.

After they moved away to Mt. Pleasant, I went to stay a week with her. They lived in a park and all you had to do was walk down an oil road to get to the swimming pool. Her parents worked and we were always at home alone. One day it was pouring down rain and we decided to walk to the swimming pool. It had rained for several days and in order to get to the swimming pool, we had to cross a bridge that had no railings. Even though water was running across the bridge, we felt that we could walk through the water to the other side.

As we started across the bridge, we were both swept away by the water. Winnie could swim pretty good and I thought I could swim too, but when you are trying to swim against raging water, it did not go so well. I was able to get on Winnie's back and she kept going under the water. We were lucky enough to get to a tree and I just grabbed the tree for dear life and held on. Luckily, someone from the swimming pool area saw us and came to help. They rescued her first and then came for me. And would you believe, I was hanging on a tree with a big snake. I know this does not sound possible, but it is true.

Since we could not go back home, someone took us to where her parents worked and left us. We were in big trouble until we told them what had happened and then I think they were just thankful we had not drowned. Anyhow, we learned a good lesson about trying to cross a bridge in raging water. I never told my parents about this because this would have ended my visiting her in Mt. Pleasant.

We then had another rich family move into the house they moved out of. The Manleys owned part of the Dodge Plymouth Dealership in town and had two daughters, Sharon and Carla. Sharon was my age and so I had a new friend. These kids even had braces on their teeth, so I knew they were rich. However, this made no difference to me; if they would just play with me, they were okay. They even ate different food than we ate and often asked me to stay for dinner. We had baby cabbages and they called them cauliflower. Their kids hated them, but I thought they were quite cute and tasty. Of course, if it was food, it was good to me because I loved to eat, but not as much as I loved to play.

As I was growing up, I not only had a loving mother and daddy, but I also had an older man and woman, (Mr. and Mrs. Gurley a/k/a Uncle Ed and Ms. Gurley) who lived just down the hill from us in a small one-room white house with a front porch and flat-hoed yard. I think they did have a small kitchen with an ice box, but no bedrooms separate from where they lived. They did not have indoor plumbing, which was nice because when I spent the night with them, we had a slop jar under the bed and we just had to crawl out of bed and use it and crawl back into bed.

My sister and I had a little red boy's bicycle that I'm sure was hers, and she just let me ride it. Nannie did not have much to do with them and did love to mess up their yard. She would come flying down the hill on that little red bicycle and slide sideways in their flat-hoed yard that they kept smooth and spotless and then ride off. Of course, they did not like that; not even a little bit.

I loved makeup, but mother did not like for me to get into her makeup, so I knew better than to bother it. She would give me the little lipstick samples from Avon, but those did not last long. If I needed or wanted makeup, Uncle Ed would walk to town and would always come back with me a tube of lipstick or some fingernail polish and sometimes both. He even bought me the cutest little red and white heart-shaped valentine pin that I thought was just beautiful. I still have it to this day and will always treasure it.

My daddy always called me his little "PP" girl, standing for primp and play. This was before the girlfriends moved away and I had to become a tomboy and play football with the neighbor boys (Billy, Cliff, Randy and Gary), and my dear friend, Jean Shirley.

The Shirleys lived behind us and their land was adjacent to ours when we lived in the little white house on the hill. They had three sons, Vernon, Kenneth, and Rex, and one daughter, Jean, who I loved to play with. I can remember Kenneth out plowing behind a horse with a hand-held plow and I would sit at the fence and watch him. He would always chew plug tobacco when he plowed and every time he would come by and would take a bite, I would tell him that I had never had any chewing tobacco and wanted to try it. He finally broke down and gave me his plug of tobacco and told me to take a bite. I took a bite and within a few minutes, I was a pretty sick girl and had to go to the house. I think I was turning green, and Mother kept asking me what was wrong and I finally told her that I had begged Kenneth for some chewing tobacco and he let me have a bite. I think Mother just thought I got what I deserved, but didn't say it.

The Shirleys were probably every bit as poor as we were because they lived in a big two story house that they had partially finished and had the rafters showing in a lot of the rooms, but I loved spending time at their house. Most of the time Jean would come to my house and play because until I was older, Mother would not let me go to her house and play because her mother worked and was always gone. Ruben, her dad, was usually there, but was always working in the garden or the field and Mother did not think he would watch us closely enough. However, this was okay as long as I could play with Jean.

After the Manleys moved to town in a house behind their car dealership we were just like the Jeffersons, and moved on up. We moved to the brick mansion on the hilltop where the Robbs and the Manleys had lived. I thought this house was the most beautiful house and it even had a bathtub and a wall heater with carpet on the floors. Of course my sister and I still had to share a bedroom with the bed with the imaginary line down the middle. I was sad to lose my playmates, but was happy to be living where they had lived. We moved up the hill one piece of furniture at a time, just like little pissants, but we were skipping all the way. Did this mean we were now rich? I'm afraid not, but we didn't know the difference. The only difference I could see was that they had store-bought clothes and Mother made ours. I thought ours were just as cute as theirs.

When we moved to the brick house on the hill, the Shirleys lived just in our backyard, except for a fence which was easy enough to go around, so this made Jean accessible to me at any time. We were almost inseparable. She had to clean house and do lots of chores, and I would help her just so I could be with her. Her dad would cook dinner at night since her mother worked and was not at home during the day. Many times they would ask me to stay for dinner and mother would let me. Her dad made the best beef stew and cornbread. The stew would have big chunks of potatoes and carrots and onions and was so good. I was always glad to help with the dishes.

Jean and I loved to play football with the neighborhood boys that were much younger than we were. We would play almost every day after school. Her room in this big red house was upstairs and was not completed at all, but we loved it up there. I would even get to spend the night occasionally and we would laugh and talk all night long. We even decided that we needed to become blood sisters, so we got us a needle and pricked our fingers and became blood sisters.

Her oldest brother, Vernon, drove a chicken truck and tried to sleep in the daytime. He would let me rub his back while he fell asleep and I would just sit on the bed and watch him sleep. I loved him and was going to marry him someday. However, there was a small problem, and that was that he was much older than me and had a girlfriend named Patricia. I always assured him that it was okay to date her, but I wanted him to wait until I grew up so I could marry him. He always assured me that he would. However, before I knew it, he was going to marry Patricia and leave me. My heart was broken. I went to their wedding and cried all through the wedding. Not a little cry, but a boo-hoo sobbing cry. This was definitely my first heartbreak. Her other two brothers were really good looking, but they were just like brothers to me. They called me "Little Judge" and when I started to high school, this name followed me. They would call me this on the school bus and the rest of the kids started calling me this. I was then known around town as "Little Judge." Believe me, that was okay with me because I adored my daddy.

While we were living in the brick house on top of the hill, we got our first television set. It was black and white and the neighborhood kids would come to watch TV. We would all gather around right in front of it and watch whatever was on. I can remember Art Linkletter, and Bonanza, but that is about the only two shows I remember until the Mickey Mouse Club and American Bandstand with Dick Clark and we were all hooked.

Mother bought my sister and me a piano and arranged for us to take lessons from Mrs. Petty in town. She would sit on the stool right beside you and click her false teeth all during the lesson, and that would have been okay, but she also required us to practice at home and that did it for me. The only thing I liked about the piano lessons was the recitals and the beautiful formals that we wore to the recitals. I did not like practicing so I did not excel in this field. I had rather be outside playing so Mother decided she was just wasting her money on me. My sister continued with her lessons because she didn't mind practicing at home and she became a good piano player. She was asked to be in a beauty contest and that was her talent. Of course, I had no beauty and no talent, because I just wanted to play outside. My favorites were playing football and riding bicycles. You would think with all the exercise that I got that I would not be fat, but this was not the case. I was bigger around than I was tall. As I look back, I can understand how that happened because there were many nights that I had at least two dinners and sometimes three. I would be asked to eat with whoever I was playing with at dinnertime, and seldom turned down a meal. Mother cooked lunch because Daddy came to the house for lunch and then we would have leftovers for dinner. We would come home from school and the food would still be on the top of the stove and we would always have to check it out, so a lot of times we didn't have too much left for supper. Daddy didn't care because he would just fix him some soft boiled eggs and eat them on bread. They always looked so good when he was eating them, but one bite later, I knew this was not for me. Of course, there were times when we would have biscuits, sausage and gravy for dinner and I would eat my fair share of this.

Chapter 2

When I was old enough to go to school, I had a rough start. In the first grade I had a teacher, Mrs. Caperton, that loved to spank. Every Monday I would tell my Mother that I didn't want to go to school and when she asked why, I told her "I ain't gonna be nothing nohow." Of course, that didn't work, so I had to go to Plan B, i.e., sick. After Mother made me stay in bed all day while she went to the wash room in the garage and washed, I quickly found that that didn't work, so decided to just go ahead and go to school. I was so afraid of this teacher that I hated the first grade. My very first spanking that I can remember was from her. She would spank us if we missed a word in reading. My first spanking was because I missed the word "happy." I pronounced it "hoppy" and got my lick for it.

I stayed in trouble with her a lot because I had a friend that stuttered, Marsha Wiley, and she would try to call my name to get my attention and by the time she got my name out, I was in trouble for answering her.

One day this teacher told us that we were not to disturb her no matter what and I needed to go to the restroom, but I knew better than to ask. I then decided to squat down and clean out my little desk and, of course, when I squatted down I peed the floor. She was so angry with me because I didn't ask to go to the restroom that she made me and my friend, Glynda Underwood, go and get the mop and mop it up. I also had to wear some boys coveralls the rest of the day because I was so fat that nothing else would fit me. Needless to say, this was her only year to teach at Winnsboro, but I was already warped. Poor Benny Blundell always had wet pants because he was spanked by her every day in reading class. We all felt sorry for him.

Even though we just lived a mile and a half out of town, we got to ride the school bus. The bus would pass our house and go down to Winkle's Grocery and turn around and then we were the last to get on. The bus driver, Mr. Rogers, would just pick me up and sit me on the heater right beside him. I was pretty little and he didn't want the big kids bothering me, I guess. Or perhaps, there were no seats left.

I then was lucky enough to have the best teacher ever in the second grade, Mrs. Alewine. She was so nice that I decided to keep going to school and loved it. I don't remember much about the second grade except we were having trouble with my best friend, Dina. She did not want to go to school because she was not in my classroom. It really upset me because I loved her so much and knew she needed to be in school. After a while, they finally moved her to my classroom and she was fine. I think the real reason she didn't want to go to school was because she was afraid something would happen to her mother while she was at school and she didn't want to leave her. We both always had a fear of losing our parents.

We then went on to the 3rd grade with another nice teacher, Mrs. Foster. It was in this grade that a sweet little shy girl moved from Dallas to Winnsboro, and we then had a new friend. She was so cute and we all loved her and still do to this day. She lived on a dairy farm and had such unique parents. In their eyes, we could do no wrong. They would let us drive the pickup in the pasture as we grew older. Her daddy would always bring her a glass of milk to bed and tell her goodnight and I thought that was so special. Of course, I did not like milk, so it didn't bother me that I didn't get any milk. She had a little brother that I thought couldn't walk because his mother and daddy carried him around all the time. I soon learned that he could walk, but loved to be babied and was spoiled rotten. When I would ride the school bus home with her to spend the night, he would always walk down the dirt road and meet us. I think one of my fondest memories at her house was when we were sitting at the table working on Valentine cards and we wanted to give money and all we had was a dollar bill. Needless to say the only way we could split it was to cut it in half and give half to one person and the other half to another. We always liked to give gifts.

Unfortunately, she had to learn there was no Santa Claus because of me. Her parents drove her to my house one Christmas Eve late to deliver a gift to me and, lo and behold, my parents had my Santa presents on the front porch waiting for me to go to sleep. I think that was the year I got a bicycle for Christmas. In case you haven't figured out who this was, it was Linda Nichols Brewer, who to this day is a very dear friend of mine.

This was the year that I had my very first real boyfriend, Tim McKendry. Because of being so short, I always had the smallest desk in the classroom, with a lot less storage space than everybody else. I always sat at the front of the classroom; I thought because of my size, but now I'm wondering if it wasn't because of the way I behaved, i.e., always talking and laughing. Tim sat in the back of the classroom and we always got into trouble for throwing kisses to each other. One day Ms. Foster threatened to move Tim into the desk with me if we didn't stop. Of course that would not have been good because there was no room for him in that small desk, so we immediately stopped. My daddy's expression for this boyfriend was that he could eat peas out of a fruit jar; I think because of his front teeth.

Then comes the fourth grade with another good teacher, Mrs. Black. She wasn't much to look at and was sort of gruff, but was very nice. We all had a lot of respect for her because of her gruffness, but she had a very kind heart. She made the class interesting because she taught woodworking. We got to cut out our own pattern and then sand and varnish it and put it together. I made a pony pulling a cart and was so proud of it. As a matter of fact, I still have it to this day.

In the 5th grade I had another good teacher, Ms. Helen Alvis. This year my boyfriend was Ted Beaty. We wrote notes and passed them back and forth during class. My daddy always liked to tease me about my boyfriends. He told me one day that the City had sued Ted's mother because her butt was too close to the sidewalk. She was very short, but such an admirable lady raising three sons alone. They lived over by the ballpark and walked everywhere they went because I don't think they had a car.

As I progressed in school, it was pretty much downhill from here on through the 8th grade. I had a teacher named Ms. Rucker that nobody seemed to like. If the truth be known, I was probably bullied in middle school, but we didn't know anything about bullying and I sure never realized I was being bullied. For instance, there was my boyfriend, James Samson that started calling me "Baby Elephant" and everybody picked up on it and that was my new nickname.

I decided that since Mother didn't have much money that I could help out by working in the lunchroom and earning a free lunch. In order to do this, you had to wear a hairnet, which certainly did not help my looks. The kids coming through the line would make fun of me for working in the lunchroom and wearing a hairnet. I didn't really care because I just knew I was helping our family out.

In the 7th grade I wanted to be in the band, but in order to be in the band, you had to buy your own instrument. Heaven knows, we could not afford this, but luckily if you played the drums you didn't have to buy them, so this is what I did. Another case of bullying was that we wore Bobbie socks and had to continue wearing them even when the elastic was gone if they did not have holes in them. Most all of my friends would wear rubber bands around theirs to hold them up, but my legs were so fat that the rubber bands would cut the circulation off, so I had to just let them droop. Everybody made fun of me because my socks were drooping down over my shoes. We were not allowed to wear pants to school and had to wear dresses or skirts and blouses, so you can imagine how cute this was.

In the 7th grade, I was bigger around than I was tall so I decided in order to look better, I needed glasses. I went to Sulphur Springs with the Dodgens to see the eye doctor, Dr. Crawford. I told them I needed to have my eyes checked also and this doctor never gave up an opportunity to put somebody in glasses, so I went home with glasses with very colorful frames. I guess my Mother paid the Dodgens for the glasses. The next week at school we had pictures taken. My mother told me before I left home to not wear the glasses when I had my picture taken. She dressed me in a pretty blouse and quilted skirt that she had made, with matching shoes. While I was standing in line to get my picture taken, I decided the glasses would make me look so much better, so I got out of line and ran to the classroom to get my new glasses. When I got home from school, my Mother asked me if I wore the glasses in the picture and I told her yes. She said that was fine, we just would not buy the pictures, which broke my heart. When it came time to buy the pictures, I guess she had a change of heart and let me buy them.

SCHOOL DAYS 1956-57

While I was in middle school, I had a friend named Glynda Underwood that lived with her grandparents, Opel and Tilford Moore, on Blackjack Street, which was right by the baseball park. She had a pink bicycle that we called the "pink Cadillac." I would pump her all over town on this bicycle. I loved spending the night with her because we could go to the baseball games. Her granddad worked at the concession stand, so we could get in free.

Speaking of baseball, this is another sport I attempted. I was on a team and was so fat Mother had to make my black shorts for my black shorts and white T-shirt uniform. I played shortstop and one night when I bent down, I ripped the whole seat out of my shorts. This didn't stop me from playing even though my whole butt was sticking out. Everybody teased me because when I would hit the ball and try to run, it was like I was running in place and never made it to first base. No matter how much I was teased, I still loved playing.

In the 8th grade we had many teachers and had to change classrooms. My homeroom teacher was Ms. Baber, who also taught my English class. She would sit on the radiator next to my desk and peck me on the head with a yardstick for no reason at all. I did not care for her too much and neither did my mother and daddy. Mr. Fink was my Math teacher and Mr. Ragsdale was my Geography teacher. They were very nice. In the 8th grade we got to leave school for lunch and would walk to town and eat at Martin's Drugstore or go to Greenlee's for a hamburger.

I also played basketball in the 8th grade, but was not too good at that either. My boyfriend was Tommy Hollingsworth. We were in the band together and he played the saxophone. Daddy said his parents left him out too long and he mildewed; this was because he had a lot of freckles.

I never made good grades in school, something like B's and C's while my sister made straight A's. However, my mother and daddy never did get onto me about my grades in anything but Citizenship. I think they realized that I wasn't the sharpest tack on the board, but felt I could at least behave in class. I believe I had a condition that was unknown at the time; i.e., ADD. In addition to having ADD, I had a condition that made me laugh a lot resulting in the C's in Citizenship. I was a very happy little girl and everything seemed to be funny to me.

Sundays were mostly fun days for me when I was a little girl. Mother and Daddy went to church at a Primitive Baptist Church at Good Hope, which was usually a dreadful day for me because we would have to sit for hours and listen to three or four preachers, which lasted way past lunchtime. The men would get to go outside and smoke a cigarette, but the women and children had to sit through it all. A lot of times we would have what they called dinner on the ground, which sometimes made it worth the wait. I had many pinches while sitting all this time and listening to these preachers. Thank goodness they only had church once a month.

On Sundays that we did not go to church, we would load up and go to my Uncle Dewey and Aunt Gertrude's house on Sunday afternoon to visit with them and my granddaddy and grandmother. They had a daughter, Nelda, for me to play with and Aunt Gertrude many times had tea cakes or cold cornbread to eat and we knew where to look for them. If we didn't go there, we would go to Uncle Buddy's and Aunt Evie's and they had two daughters, Sara and Pamela. My sister played with Sara and I played with

Pamela and we always had a good time. Pamela and I would play house and make mud pies. They also lived on an oil road and we would go on walks up the road.

When my sister and I were a little older, she and I started going to the First Baptist Church. Mother and Daddy did not go with us but Mother would take us and pick us up. We went to Sunday School and Church and then back to Training Union and Church in the evening. We usually got home in time to watch Bonanza on Sunday nights. I was also in the GA's and reached the highest rank. We had a wonderful teacher, Louise Taylor, Susie's grandmother. She and her husband had a cabin at Lake Franklin and she would take us there for slumber parties.

At the age of 12, I was saved. I was to be baptized that Sunday night and was scared to death to tell my parents because they did not really agree with the belief that you had to be baptized. I went home from Church and decided if I told my daddy, he would convince Mother it was okay. He went to the barn to milk and I followed him, with only a few hours left before time for me to go back to Church. I was just about to tell him when a cow got out and he kicked at the cow and fell flat on his butt. I didn't think it was a good time to tell him until he cooled off. I finally got up the nerve and told him and he seemed pleased. He even went to Church with me that evening for the baptism.

My daddy also loved to sing and we spent a lot of Sunday afternoons going to what we called "singings." There were song books that we sang from and people would take turns leading the singing. It was usually the same people there and my daddy loved it. Mother did not enjoy it nearly as much but would go along most of the time. I think the thing she hated most about it was the many times we would get lost on the way. We always had to try a new route and would get lost. Besides that, my daddy always loved to see new territory and when he would look away from the road, the car would veer off the road and scare Mother. If he passed a driveway, he would go ahead and turn in anyhow making us go into the ditch. He didn't think it was a problem because he would just drive right out of it.

Later my granddaddy and grandmother moved to town and lived on Pine Street. My grandmother died when I was very young, so I can't remember much about her, but that she would sit in her bedroom and rock in her rocking chair and dip snuff. She would give us her little snuff cans and we would make snuff out of cocoa and sugar and pretend we were dipping. My granddaddy and grandmother did not drive, but he bought her a new Chevrolet that sat in the garage. The only time it was driven was when one of the boys or mother would drive them somewhere.

My Aunt Eunice and her husband, Kenneth, lived with my grandparents in town and they had two adorable children, Cheryl Kay and John. We went to their house often and Mother would always make it back to the kitchen to see what good was on the stove for her to eat. Cheryl and John were very young at the time, but we always played. There was a little store just around the corner from them run by Mr. Spearman and we would often get to go there and get some candy. I remember one time John swallowed a jawbreaker and Eunice held him upside down and shook him until it came out. It really scared all of us. From then on, we were not allowed to buy jawbreakers.

After Eunice and Kenneth moved to Mount Vernon and my granddaddy lived alone, Mother would go by every day and check on him and make sure he had food to eat. She would even clean his house. He would let me mow the yard and give me $5.00, which was a lot of money to me.

My daddy's parents lived in Anadarko, Oklahoma in a big white house with Aunt Syble and Jim and I loved visiting them. It was a real trip to go and visit them and we would spend the night, and sometimes more than one night. My granddaddy would let me stand on the top of his shoes and he would walk me up and down the sidewalk. They lived real close to the place that they had the Indian shows with real live Indians. My Aunt Syble was quite the entertainer and would always take us to the park, the Western Union office where she worked and even to the movies. My granddaddy was a tall man with black hair and a black moustache. I don't remember too much about him because they lived so far away that we didn't see them very often and then he died while I was still in grade school. My grandmother was a tall woman but was a little on the hefty side and loved to sit and rock. She wore big dresses that always hung on her and wore her gray hair pulled back in a bun. She would take it down at night and brush it. I was always a little afraid of her because she spoke her mind and made no bones about it. I don't think she really liked my mother that much and I think the feelings were probably mutual. However, she had a contagious laugh and laughed quite often and I always loved to hear her laugh. My daddy always loved to go there and especially loved spending time with Aunt Syble because they were so very close. I loved playing with Jim and he always had some kind of game or magic trick to show me. He was much older than me, but loved to entertain me. After my granddaddy died, Aunt Syble was transferred to Ada, Oklahoma with Western Union and lived in a brick house with a little wooden shed out back that Jim and I spent a lot of time in. He had everything you would need to entertain you in that little shed.

The trips to Oklahoma were quite exciting because my daddy did not believe in going anywhere the same way you had gone before and even came home a different way. He would get us lost quite often and this drove Mother crazy. He didn't mind getting lost, and she hated it.

If Mother didn't go with us, Uncle Hy, Daddy and I would go and that was always real exciting. Uncle Hy had to go to the bathroom a lot and we would stop beside the road and he would go behind a tree and use the bathroom. He cursed like a sailor and always wanted Daddy to stop for gas because he damn sure wasn't going to walk. The three of us got lost once when Daddy was trying a new route. We ended up in a little town and Daddy stopped and Uncle Hy asked a man where in the hell we were. The man asked him where he wanted to be and I thought this was so very funny, even though I was scared to death because I knew we were lost. These were always very exciting trips, but we would have a good time.

My daddy wore a hat and was always leaving it at the cafe when we would stop to eat and we would always have to turn around and go back to get it. However, it didn't matter because we were on a trip and having fun. Besides that, I always loved to stop and eat and usually ordered chicken fried steak.

The only family vacation we ever took was to Carlsbad, New Mexico to see Carlsbad Caverns. This was the trip of the lifetime for a little country girl that had never been on a vacation. We stayed in Best Western Motels and I thought this was the ultimate. I would stand up in the floorboard of the back seat and brush and curl my daddy's hair while he drove. Of course we stopped and ate on the way in cafes and that was exciting. I guess the reason we never got to go on another vacation was because I asked a thousand times, "Are we almost there?" The caverns were unbelievable and a bit scary because we were told that bats lived in them. Of course I could have done without them telling me this. As far as I was concerned, it would have been right next to them telling me the devil lived there. I think, but I'm not sure, that my sister even enjoyed this vacation.

We did not feel cheated because we did not take family vacations because we knew this was something that only rich people did.

Mother and I took the train to Midland, Texas to visit Dick and Annalou Bass. These were friends of Mother and Daddy when he worked in the oilfield. I thought they were rich because they had a beautiful brick home, and treated us like royalty. I was kind of scared at their house though because I could hear sirens and this was something I was not used to hearing. I thought they were coming after us every time I would hear them. They would take Mother to Odessa to visit other friends that she and daddy were good friends with. One lady was named Nona and the only thing I remember about her was that she lived in a little stucco house and had a little dog. Mother had just gotten false teeth before we went to Midland and during the night she lost her teeth in her sleep. She was so upset because she thought she swallowed them. Believe it or not, we found them under the bed.

On the train trip, we had to change trains in Dallas and Mother had me carrying the little suitcase and we were running from train to train trying to find the right train and I dropped the little suitcase and underwear flew everywhere. This really did put Mother in a tizz. I think it turned out that we had gotten off the train that we really needed to be on.

I was such an innocent and naïve little girl with such a loud mouth that really never meant any harm, but I think my sister just did not appreciate my mouth and had a little trouble surviving around me. This prefaces the story of the morning I ran down the hill to wait on the school bus with the other kids and it was a morning after it had rained the night before. The hill I ran down was a clay hill and at the bottom of the hill, I found two dogs stuck together rear to rear. Common sense would tell you that they were stuck together with clay, so I quickly started working on getting them apart. I sent Billy and Cliff to their house to get some hot water to pour on them and another kid to get a pair of scissors. We worked diligently, but did not have enough time before the bus arrived. As soon as the bus driver, Edgar Turner, opened the door, I rushed on in a panic to tell him about the two dogs stuck together and asked if he could help us get them apart. My sister had just arrived and gotten in line to get on the bus when she heard me telling Mr. Turner about our problem. She quickly peeled out of line and rushed to the house to tell Mother what I was saying and refused to ever ride the school bus again. Needless to say, from this day forward Mother had to drive her to school. Of course I still rode the bus because that was one of my highlights of the day in going to school. Once again, I probably thought dogs went down into the pasture and found puppies. The only thing that puzzles me to this day is how my sister was raised by the same parents and knew more than I did. I guess it was because she was almost two years older than me.

In the 8th grade, I fell in love with Paul Garrison and because of him, I managed to lose weight and was told by my friend. Claudia Mullinax. that if I would get a manicure and pedicure, he would probably ask me out. Needless to say, I did not know what either of those were, but luckily he asked me to go on a church trip to Tyler bowling and I was so happy. My mother bought me a new Peter Pan padded bra from Miss Inman's dress shop (which was later the Fashion Shop) and boy was this a mistake because when he hugged me, the bra stayed crushed in and I had little crushes that I had to punch back out. The best part about the whole trip was that he kissed me and that was it. I was not in love with him and actually did not even want to go on a date with him. Not that he asked me, but it no longer mattered. I was over him.

We did not have much money when I was growing up so Mother made most all our clothes. We did have petticoats that were probably store bought and Mother starched them so they would really stand out. The only problem with this was that my sister got to wear them until they went limp, and then it was my turn. Of course I didn't need them because I was about as round as I was tall. My shirts always gapped in the front if they were store bought. When Mother would tell me that we didn't have enough money to buy something, I would always tell her to write a check. Needless to say, I didn't know that you had to have money to write a check.

The only time I ever heard my mother and daddy disagree on anything was when I overheard them arguing and I heard Daddy say that he would just leave home. For days I followed him around and even sat outside the bathroom door when he was in there. I was so afraid he was going to leave. I didn't know at the time what it was all about, but shortly after that Daddy went into business for himself. He opened a used tractor and tractor supply shop down at the milk barn and had a little office out front. I think as I look back on it that this is what they were arguing about. I am pretty sure we did not have the money for him to do this. Mother had a little income from some oil money that granddaddy had given her and this was the only income they had after Daddy quit working for Pat Campbell.

Mother would work at the Livestock barn on Fridays making hamburgers along with Aunt Myrtie. In the summertime I would help by serving them while they made them on the grill.

As I said, my daddy had a little shop in front of the barn where he ran his used tractor and parts business. If he had to run to town he would let me run it and I really felt important. I would be so happy if somebody came and bought something while he was gone because I had made money for him.

Since he sold used tractors, I learned to drive on a tractor. My daddy would let me drive the tractors anytime I wanted to. He also had me help him unload the tractors off the trailer by driving them off and when you would get to the bottom, the tractor would rear straight up scaring me to death. He never got excited and would just tell me to push in on the clutch and that is all it took. He was going to teach me to mow the pasture and that did not work out either because I was to follow him and almost ran over him with the tractor.

He and I went out on the Sulphur Springs Highway to pick up a tractor with a hay mower on it. He wanted me to drive the tractor home while he followed me in the truck. This did not work out so well either because I mowed down several mail boxes on the way home that he had to contact the people and repair and/or replace. He never got upset over anything I did, and would make me so proud by telling people I was his little helper.

My first car to drive was a Buick Roadster with power steering. After driving tractors, the first driving lesson was not too good. Daddy let me drive to Dina's house with him riding with me. The power steering was throwing me off and I could hardly keep the car out of the ditch. The real kicker was when I had to turn into the driveway, which was pretty narrow with a culvert. I only ran off with the back tire and once again, Daddy bragged on me and said I was a good driver.

While I was in middle school, I was able to join the Camp Fire Girls led by Ms. Suiter. We worked hard on fundraisers and earning our little buttons for our vests. We would go on long hikes and did so many things together.

The summer after entering High she took us on a trip to Washington, D.C. where we met and got our picture taken with Lyndon B. Johnson. My Mother went on the trip with us. As a matter of fact, we had many chaperones. We were all so excited because we were going on a Greyhound Bus, which none of us had been on a bus trip before. We all were anxiously awaiting the bus out on the sidewalk in front of her house on North Main Street when this old, old purple bus came pulling up. We didn't know it at the time, but they had sent this bus to pick us up and take us to Texarkana where we would take the Greyhound. We named the bus the grape juice can. As best I remember, it broke down before we even got to Texarkana. This was a trip of a lifetime but because we were not into government and history, we did not grasp a lot of adventures she took us on. At the time we were just into boys and I think she had us booked into "all girl" hotels. Once we were checked into our rooms, we were not allowed out except to go to dinner. Believe me, she kept a close eye on us and we had a lot of respect for her.

Chapter 3

Freshman and Sophomore Pictures

Junior and Senior Pictures

Once we entered High School, we were promoted to the Horizon Club which she also sponsored. Ms. Suiter was not married and lived in a large house on North Main. She was a lawyer by day and we were her girls. She wanted us to experience so many things and even fixed cow tongue for dinner for us one night. It was so good, but once she told us what it was we could not eat another bite. I could just feel myself chewing on a cow tongue.

She brought us to Dallas to go to the Majestic Theater to see Around The World in 80 Days on the big screen that was amazing to all of us.

She took us to Galveston to the beach and did so much for us. But she always had her eye on us.

My high school years were filled with fun. After losing weight, I finally started dating. My first real boyfriend and first real car date was with Lynn Swanner. We went to the movies on a Sunday afternoon to see The Ten Commandments. We dated through the 9th grade and into the 10th grade. The only other dates I had during this time were with Kathy Parker's cousin, Steve Simms, who lived in Dallas and would come to visit her and we would have dates. I also had a date with a really cute guy that I can't remember his name, but I remember he drove an old car, which didn't really matter. I just remember saying I was going to roll the window down and when I tried, the window didn't budge, so I told him I didn't really want it down. I think the roller was broken, or something. I didn't have a very good time with him, so never went on another date with him. Perhaps he didn't even ask me for another date. Anyhow, I started going steady with Lynn Swanner. We dated the remainder of my Freshman year and into my Sophomore year.

During the summer of my Freshman year we all loaded into Sandra Swanner's Mercury and went to Tyler State Park for July 4th. My Mother did not want me to go but finally agreed to let me go. While there, Sandra and I decided to slide down the big slide double with her going first and me holding onto her. At the bottom my head hit her elbow, or something, and the next thing I knew the lifeguard was pulling me out of the lake.

My head was bleeding profusely, so they laid me with my feet above my head and put ice on my head. When the bleeding stopped they agreed to let Sandra drive me to Mother Frances Hospital in Tyler. We all unloaded at the hospital in our bathing suits and they took me to the Emergency Room and took 12 stitches in my head. As far as I know, they never contacted my parents about insurance information before treating me, but just treated and released me. By the time we got home my face was swollen and both eyes were black and blue. Mother and Daddy were having a stew with all of the neighbors at our house and my Mother almost passed out when she saw me. Believe it or not, I did not get into trouble. I think she was just thankful that I was still alive.

During the summer of my sophomore year, my friend Clara and her boyfriend Jerry wanted to introduce me to a boy from Perryville that was friends with Jerry, and so I went on a blind date with J. D. I don't know why I went because I think I was still supposed to be going steady with Lynn.

I must go into detail here about my friend Clara. She and I had been friends since we were very young. Her daddy and my daddy both loved to sing and we would go to singing conventions, as well as singing schools together. She was older than me, but always made me laugh and was so much fun.

On our blind date, we went to a Rodeo and I had on a straight skirt that made it hard for me to climb the bleachers. We did have a good time, but J.D. mumbled and it was hard for me to understand a word he said. The only thing I really liked about him other than the fact that he was good looking was that he really knew how to kiss. However, I did not really care if I ever had another date with him because I did like Lynn a lot. J.D. asked me for a date and I think I said I would go even though I didn't really want to until one of my friends said he had asked her for a date the same night. When we were riding the streets in town the next week and saw the Perryville boys, I flagged him down and asked him who he had a date with and he said me hopefully. That is when we really started dating. I didn't particularly want the date but I sure didn't want anybody else going out with him. That was the beginning of our relationship. The most impressive thing about him was that he would take me to a movie and buy me a coke and popcorn. When I was dating Lynn, I often had to pay my own way into the movie and if I wanted a coke and popcorn, I had to buy my own. It was fun to go on a date and not pay your own way.

When J.D. and I started dating, we had a collie named Tinker. One night when he came to pick me up and got out of the car, Tinker bit him in the butt and he didn't care too much for that dog from then on.

We dated through high school and the only time I had other dates was when he would get jealous and break up with me. I would then have a date or two and we would be back together. I then found out he went out with one of my friends that went to Dallas while he was living in Dallas and I broke up with him. I was asked for a date by a friend of his from Perryville, Wayne McAlister, and went out with him. J. D. happened to be in town and saw us and followed us all night long. We were then back together again and shortly after that we became engaged. He gave me a ring for my 16th birthday, with the understanding that we would not get married until I got out of high school. He was in college at East Texas and was only home on the weekends.

While he was in college at East Texas was the only time in my life that I ever did anything when my daddy told me no. This was when I went to the Sulphur Springs Drive-In to meet him during the week. When J.D. found out I was not supposed to be there because my daddy told me not to go, he immediately sent me home because he was also afraid of my daddy. My daddy was such an easy going man, but when he said no, he meant no. J.D. was afraid we would both be in trouble.

Even though I was dating J.D. in high school, I had a lot of fun with my friends. These friends were Dina, Linda, Mary, Susie, Kathy, Claudia, Linda Gibson, Sue Johnson, and others at times, that all ran around together.

I was in Homemaking for 4 years in High School and Ms. Smith and Mrs. Thompson would take us on Homemaking Trips. We came to a convention in Dallas and stayed at the old Sheraton Hotel. There was a girl that stayed in our room named Carolyn Bradley that we didn't know very well, but knew she was Jehovah Witness. She told us that she could speak in the unknown tongue and we kept begging her to do it for us. She said we would all have to pray and if she received the spirit, she could do it. So, needless to say, we agreed to pray with her. All of a sudden, the Holy Spirit took over and she began talking in the unknown tongue. It was very loud and I think the people in the room next to us must have complained because our teachers came knocking on the door. We shoved her into a closet, but could not stop her. We told the teachers what had happened and of course we were in trouble. Finally, she quieted down and what a relief it was. We were afraid we were going to get kicked out of the hotel.

Another Homemaking trip was to New Orleans. We went to Pontchartrain Beach and rode the roller coaster and then went on a dinner cruise. While on the cruise we talked Claudia, who looked older than us, into going to the bar and buying a beer. She put the beer in her large purse and carried it back to the motel where we were staying. We iced it down in the lavatory and when it was cold enough, we all gathered in one room and took turns taking a sip out of the bottle. You would have thought we had drank a keg of beer because we were talking ninety-to-nothing and dying laughing. Once again, teachers knocking on the door.

Trip to New Orleans

We took this trip on a school bus and all the way there Dina wanted to use my pillow that I had brought. I thought in order to solve this, we would just take her a pillow from the motel and she could use it on the way home. I think a lot of the group had the same idea because the next week after we were back in school the teachers got a letter from the motel where we stayed with a list of items that were taken that needed to be returned. Since I had taken the pillow for Dina, I had to own up to it and return it to the teachers. Once again, I was in trouble with my mother who was very embarrassed because she knew that I knew better than to take something from a motel.

For a brief period of time, my daddy worked at the Buick Dealership. While he was working there, he bought my sister and me a little orange and white Opel. This car was more fun than you can imagine. We would all load up in it and ride the streets of Winnsboro up and down Main Street and out on the Sulphur Springs Highway to the Freezette and turn around and back to Main Street. There were always boys doing the same thing, i.e., Pickton boys, Perryville boys and Winnsboro boys. If we ran low on gas, we would all pool our money and buy gas to keep on going. I taught most of my friends how to drive in this little Opel that was standard shift and Daddy couldn't figure out why we went through so many clutches. In the summertime, we would all load in and go to an alum Pool out on the Coke Road for a swim in our underwear. I could elaborate on this, but we won't go into that.

Opel was such a fun car and we are lucky to have survived our adventures in it. We even discovered it could fly when we would go fast over the railroad track by the old cotton gin just before you got to the Sulphur Springs Highway. We did that many times and would be airborne several feet, or yards, before landing. There was another time when we decided to go across a big gravel pile out at the Y on the Sulphur Springs Highway. However, we made it to the top and then the car hit dead center and we were stuck. After being unable to get it off the gravel pile, I had to call Daddy to come and get us off. Surprisingly enough, he did not even ask how we got on top of it. I guess he just knew everything. Probably because he had done the same things while growing up.

One of my worst classes in high school was English taught by Ms. Burkham. We always had to read books and do book reports. One of the books was the Scarlet Letter. I read the entire book, but, as usual, did not retain what I read. When it was time for me to give my book report in front of the class, she asked me about the book and I told her I thought it was a Western because they started out in a stagecoach. She was convinced that I never read the book. When I finished my book report in front of the class, or if we had to memorize something and recite it, everything was funny to me when I finished. It was that condition I had that set in once again. She finally started making me stand outside the classroom in the hallway until class was over. Believe me, I just had no control over laughing at everybody else after I finished.

I think the only class I excelled in in high school was typing and I was a very good typist until it came to taking a typing test. Once the teacher mentioned the word test, I would fall to pieces and could not even type. The rest of the time I was a very good and fast typist.

I don't know to this day how I ever got out of the Algebra class because I just never figured that out. I guess it was from the help of friends, even though I hate to admit it.

I was in the band and that entailed a lot of our activities. We would, of course, go to all of the football games and perform in many parades out of town. I played the drums, along with Barbara Crawford and Bruce Marr. My sister played the Oboe and would let me ride to band practice with her. However, I had to ride in the floorboard so her friends would not see me. I guess it was that "Big Sister" thing.

Band Pictures

Drum Corps

My Daddy loved sports and would take me and my friends to all of the out of town basketball games. We would load up in that Buick Roadster and here we would go.

After my sister graduated high school, she married Roy Hinkley and they moved to Lubbock. And would you believe, Mother and Daddy gave Opel to her, so we had no fun car. However, I had a room all to myself for the first time in my life. It was shortly after that when Daddy came home with a 1955 or '56 Chevrolet Belair for me to drive. It was not a bad looking car, but it was a gas guzzler. I ran out of gas so many times in this car that one of the boys in town, Bruce Stuart, would see me stopped on the side of the road and just go and get gas and bring it without asking if I needed help. Of course Daddy had a gas pump down at the shop that all I had to do was go and fill up at no charge, but I just couldn't find the time to do that. I had too many places to go and too many things to do.

While J.D. and I were dating, he would take me down to his house for dinner with his parents and I was so very shy. There were many funny things that happened to me when we were eating with them, but one of the funniest things I did while we were eating at the big table in the dining room. I always propped my feet on the ledge under the table and decided to scoot my chair back and turned the table over with food flying everywhere. We were all grabbing for plates and bowls of food and did a pretty good recovery job.

Mrs. Price was a very good cook and one night she had fried a platter of liver and I thought it was chicken fried steak and picked the largest piece I could find because I didn't want to ask for seconds. When I discovered that it was liver instead of steak, I was in trouble because I was much too shy to tell them that I could not eat liver, so I would cover each bite with mashed potatoes and chew it once and swallow it. I finally finished that huge piece of liver and was very careful to make sure there was no liver before I would help my plate again.

Another time, we were all there, Codell's family and us, one Sunday for lunch after church. They sat me by Mr. Price and he kept asking for more iced tea, making the comment that he didn't know where all of his tea was going. He then caught me in the act; I was drinking his tea instead of mine. He was a big jokester and loved to tease me about that for years to come. He always asked to not sit by me because I would eat his food and drink his tea.

When I started dating J.D. and he would take me around his family, they all hugged each other and would hug me too. This was so difficult for me because I was not raised in a hugging family, but I tolerated it until it became comfortable for me. I often longed for a hug from my mother and daddy, but never had a hug from my daddy.

Codell and Billy had 5 children, so there was never a dull moment. I would have some of my best laughs when we were around them because it was utter chaos. Codell was so easy going and Billy would always be out of control. He was actually very laid back but would become quite out of control when he couldn't find what he was looking for. He was quite the story teller and I would just laugh and laugh at him. Actually, he was funnier to me than any comedian I have ever seen.

My very first night club was the Longhorn Ballroom in Dallas. J.D. invited me to go with him and his stepdad, Mr. Price, to see Ray Price perform. As I had mentioned earlier, I was very shy and this was on a Sunday night. We went in the back door and they escorted us to a table that was set up for Ray's guests. I thought this was the worst place I had ever been because it was dark, dungy and very smoky. We sat at the table and Mr. Price was just beside himself because he didn't get to go and see Ray perform that often. He was having a ball and pinching the waitresses on the butt and I was just thinking if I could ever get out of that place, I would never go back. Of course, J.D. did not dance, so we just sat there the whole night until wee hours of the morning and then after seeing Ray and talking with him, we were able to leave and go home. What a night for a little innocent country girl.

While I was dating J.D., we often double-dated. My Aunt Myrtle was always telling Mother jokes and one particular joke she told they both just laughed and laughed and I did not get it and couldn't understand why it was funny.

When J.D. and I were double dating with Jack McAlister "Emmer" and Kathy Parker, I told them I had a joke to tell that my aunt had told Mother and I did not find anything funny about it. I proceeded to tell the joke and J.D. almost wrecked the car laughing and Kathy and I still did not get it. Come to find out, it was really a dirty joke and I didn't know it.

I think besides many band trips that I went on in High School (without getting into trouble) my last trip in high school was our Senior Trip to Marble Falls Lake for the day. Once again, we went on a school bus. The boys in our Senior class were all so young and innocent, but some of them decided to take liquor on the Senior trip. I have no idea how they got it, but I think it was Vodka. Since they were not drinkers, needless to say, some of them became inebriated, which was much too obvious on our bus trip home. When we stopped in Longview to eat on the way home, the teachers called the principal, Mr. Bethea, and he in turn contacted our parents and had them all meet at the school. When we arrived at the high school, we were told to get off the bus without saying a word to anyone and march directly to the auditorium. They called each one of us individually into the principal's office and questioned us as to whether we had been drinking or even had a drink before letting us go. We were told that we would not have a graduation ceremony, but I think the parents raised enough cane that we were able to graduate. As far as I know, Claudia was the only one that had a drink of all the girls but she told the principal that we had all had a drink, but she took the rap for all of us. She was Valedictorian that year and almost lost her honor, but her Dad had enough money that I think she was excused.

Senior Class

Proms

I attended my Junior and Senior Proms with J.D. We also attended his senior prom in Gilmer, which was held in a restaurant. I was playing in a little combo band at the time and we were invited to play at his prom. I can't remember who all was in it, but I know that Gay Polk sang and I played the drums. I believe Dina played the flute also.

Chapter 4

After graduating high school in June 1962, J.D. and I started discussing our wedding plans. I told him that he would have to ask my daddy and this was another story within itself. J.D. was a little afraid of my daddy; I guess because my daddy had told him all along that he needed to join the service and grow up. J.D. agreed to talk to Daddy and get his approval. It took most of the day because he could not get up the nerve to ask him.

We were married on June 21, 1962 at the First Baptist Church in Winnsboro by Brother Gray, who was a longtime friend of the Prices and had been a pastor at Perryville Baptist Church when J.D. was growing up.

We went to Greenville on our honeymoon with intentions of staying the night at a motel that I had always wanted to stay at; I believe it was called the Continental Inn. Needless to say, we did not know you had to make reservations and arrived there to find out there were no rooms available. They sent us back down the road to the Silver Spur and this is where we spent our wedding night. All I really remember about it was our room had a green door. I thought it was nice enough and after all, it was a motel and that was exciting for me. We left there the next day and drove to Dallas to visit his Aunt Neta and Uncle Clarence at Cain's Machine Shop on Elm Street in Downtown Dallas. After visiting with them, we were off to the honeymoon cottage, a one bedroom duplex on Blair Street in Mineola to start our life together. This duplex had a living room, hallway, with the bathroom off the hallway, a bedroom and then a kitchen at the back. It also had a screened-in back porch and a small fenced backyard that we shared with the neighbors. We had already moved in our living room suite that Mrs. Price had given us; the one J.D. had in his room at the old Price house, and our bedroom suite and stove and refrigerator that mother and daddy had given us, but we then had to shop for a TV and dining room suite. We managed to find one we liked and the payments were only $15.00 a month. Our rent was $30.00, so this was about all we could afford. J.D. was making $159.00 a month working at the Highway Department and I thought he was rich, but soon found out that was not a lot of money. We did not have a car payment at the time because mother had given me a car when I graduated. It was a used Pontiac that had belonged to Dr. Stuart's son and was a beautiful white car. However, J.D. did not think much of it.

Our sofa made into a bed, but when Dina would come to spend the night with us, she always wanted to sleep in the bed with J.D. and I, especially in the summertime. It could have been because we did not have air conditioning, and had only one little wooden box fan that Clara and Jerry had given us. That was in the days before air conditioning became popular and we would just sleep under a sheet with the windows open and use our one little fan all over the house.

I would get up and fix J.D. breakfast and fix his lunch and he was off to work and I was back to bed. I would sleep until time to get up to watch Days of Our Lives, which I believe came on at 11:00 or 12:00. I would then clean house and always had dinner prepared when he came home from work. He would then eat and oftentimes go to sleep and that was it for the night. I would then play solitaire until midnight or so to entertain myself. After a few months of getting up and fixing breakfast, I accidentally stuck three fingers on my right hand into hot grease while trying to put the eggs in the frying pan, and this ended my breakfast cooking. I eventually ended up putting the foil tag inside the lunch meat in J.D.'s sandwich and this ended my lunch making. No more getting up early for me.

I was not prepared for all of this cooking because Mother had never taught me to cook and the only time I was allowed in the kitchen to cook was when Mother was out town on a trip and Daddy would try to teach me to cook. He would eat what I cooked no matter if the dog would or not. I once made rock biscuits that you could break a window out with and he bragged on them. So I guess you would say I learned to cook on my own. I would get tips from other friends, i.e., boil liver before you fry it, and this did not work so well. The liver flew out of the frying pay, touched the ceiling and then came back down. It was too tough to eat, so J.D. said, but it sure left a mess on the kitchen ceiling. No more cooking liver. I then bought some frozen chicken legs and fried them frozen. They were very pretty, but when J.D. bit into them, blood squirted out. Oops, another learning experience. I had a pretty limited grocery budget and found dried pinto beans were a real bargain and J.D. always liked them, so I bought a package and cooked them. Nobody told me you had to wash them first and when we ate them, they were full of dirt and rocks. Oops yet another cooking experience. We were having company for the weekend, Jim Bob and Mary Truitt, and I went to the grocery store and found a big hen that was pretty cheap, so I bought it. I had to cut it up, but I had watched Mother do this, so I went to work on it. I fried it in my new electric skillet and it was a beautiful golden brown. We sat down to eat and could not bite into it. I later found out from Mother that you cannot fry a hen. Despite the fried hen, we had a good time with it.

We then got our first babies, two little mutts named Blackie and Whitie, real original names, huh. J.D. was bound and determined to train those two dogs and fed them so many treats trying to train them that he made them sick. He was just trying to teach them to jump up on the foot stool.

We always loaded up on the weekends and headed to Winnsboro, dogs and all. There were no fences and they just followed J.D. wherever he went. Blackie ended up getting ran over down at Daddy's shop on the busy highway. While I was gone to school one day, I left Whitie in the back yard and I think either the neighbors let her out or called the pound because when I came home, she was gone. We tried and tried to find her, to no avail. We then got another dog, part chow and part collie and named her Mitsy. The only real problem with her was that she loved cats and would roam the neighborhood collecting cats and bringing them home to us; dead, of course.

Our first Thanksgiving together was a disaster. We went to Granny and Pappas, J.D.'s grandparents, and J.D. drove our white Pontiac with Mr. and Mrs. Price in the backseat. I had met most of his relatives, but was still very shy. He left me in the house with all of those strangers while he went outside with his uncles and cousins. His uncles had brought home brew with the intention of getting J.D. drunk. He came into the house at lunchtime and when I said something to him, he just stared at me and said, "Who are you?" I was so naïve that I had no clue what was wrong with him. We then went into the dining room and J.D.'s aunts all knew what was wrong with him and they loaded his plate with cranberry sauce, which they knew he didn't like. The next thing I knew, he had turned his chair over at the table and was lying in the floor. Everybody thought it was funny except for me and Mrs. Price. We were both embarrassed and I was getting truly upset. Before we left there, he was very sick and throwing up. He rode home lying in the backseat with his head in Mrs. Price's lap and I drove with Mr. Price in the front seat. Mr. Price told everybody that I flew across the narrow bridge that had rudders without touching the bridge. I left him with his mother and Mr. Price and I went to Mothers. My Uncle Lloyd and Aunt Myrtle were there and I wanted to see them. The next time they came to Mother and Daddy's house, they brought me some Roach traps as a joke. This day was funny to everybody but me and Mrs. Price.

We did not have a telephone in our little duplex, but had a sweet little old lady and man who lived next door and they would call me to the phone if mother called. I was so used to being around my friends and having fun that I soon discovered this life was so very boring.

That's when J.D. decided that I should go to work and sent me to the First National Bank in Mineola to apply for a job. They had no openings, but every Monday J.D. insisted that I go back and check with them to see if they had any openings. I hated Mondays and I hated that bank with a passion. I'm surprised they didn't hire me so they wouldn't have to see me every Monday. I feel sure they dreaded seeing me as much as I dreaded going there. We even opened a checking account at that bank thinking it might help. This was my first checking account and, as I said earlier, we did not have much money, and certainly not enough for a checking account.

I loved it because If I didn't have money I could just write a check. That was all good until one day J.D. came home and told me he was contacted about several hot checks I had written. I told him that could not be possible because I had a lot of checks left. So much for the checking account; it was immediately closed.

Clara worked for the District Clerk in Quitman named Kelsey Ross while we were living in Mineola. She had to be off work for an extended period of time and asked Mr. Ross, who was, by the way, a singing buddy of our dads, if I could work for him while she took off and he agreed. I worked in his office for the period of time that she was off and met a really nice girl named Pat that had an adorable little girl. She worked for the District Attorney and so I had somebody to hang out with.

I then decided that maybe if I went to college and learned shorthand I would stand a better chance at getting a job. Mother offered to pay and I started Tyler Junior College and rode the bus every day and spent the whole day there just to take typing and shorthand. This was all I could afford to take. I made straight A's because I had plenty of time to get my homework while I was there. I then learned that I could walk a good distance up to the hospital and give blood and they would give me $5.00, so I started doing that to make a little money to have lunch money.

After finishing college, I still could not get a job at the bank, so I went to Piggy Wiggly and applied for a job, and believe it or not, got a job stocking shelves.

The weekend before I was to start to work on Monday, we went on a weekend trip with Clara and Jerry to Galveston. We left on Friday after they all got off work and Clara borrowed her parent's car and drove to Galveston. Her dad was handicapped and had a hand gas pedal and brake. At one point the gas got stuck on the way and we were passing everybody on the highway. We were planning on staying at the Jack Tarr right across from the beach. It was too late to get a room when we arrived, so we decided to sleep in the car on the parking lot and go to the beach the next morning. J.D., Jerry and I slept while Clara watched over us all night, as she could not sleep in the car. We were at the beach early and stayed all day long and I was as red as a lobster. Later that day, we found a man lying on the beach that had obviously been there as long as we had that was sound asleep with his "nuts" hanging out of his bathing suit. They were literally baked and after naming him "Tough Nuts," I think we decided to wake him up before they were broiled. That night we had to drive to another town to get a motel room and after checking at many different places found one that we all agreed on. By then I was sick and chilled, but we went to dinner at a nice restaurant and had a very good expensive meal (that we could barely afford). They came around with a dessert tray and I was under the impression that the dessert came with the meal, so I picked out a piece of pie that I didn't really want and then found out it was 45 cents for that piece of pie, so needless to say, I was shamed into eating the whole thing. I was really sick by then.

I started my new job on Monday and was covered in blisters and wore a blouse that rubbed them every time I moved my arms. I was miserable stocking shelves all day long. At the end of the day, I went home crying. This was just the beginning of my going home crying because the boss that I worked for followed you around all day long watching every move you made and if you made a wrong move, you would get chewed out by him. He was a real bear. However, he did like me and I was soon promoted to a checker. At least I didn't have to go the bank every Monday to check on a job and this was a real blessing. We even had light green uniforms that we wore, so I didn't have to have clothes. I just had to wash real often because I only had two uniforms. I ended up loving my job and my boss. I started out stocking shelves, and then promoted to checker, and then on to work in the office doing the payroll.

There was another small problem with Mitsy, the dog. She insisted on following me to work and would greet everybody by jumping up on the driver's door of their car when they drove up. Since she looked like a chow, nobody wanted her to greet them. My boss, Mr. Reep, would have me take her back home, but it wasn't long until she was back. We then had to start keeping her in the house and she didn't much like that.

Speaking of washing, this brings up another experience I had in early marriage. I had never washed in an automatic washing machine and didn't know what I was doing, but bought me a box of laundry detergent and a bottle of bleach and off I went to the washateria. That was the name of the laundry mats back in the 1960's. I put my clothes in two different washing machines and put laundry detergent and bleach in the one with white clothes, and colored clothes in the other. I was all set and went out to the car to sit and wait on them. It was just a matter of time when I noticed suds pouring out the front door and decided I had better check on my clothes. When I walked in the door, sure enough the suds were coming from my washing machines. I guess I had put a little too much detergent. Thank goodness it was not too busy that day, so I loaded my clothes into my laundry basket and headed home to hang them on the clothes line. That was cheaper than using the dryers and I did have a clothes line in the backyard. Heaven only knows how I could have burned the clothes up if I had used the dryer because I had never used a dryer either.

We had many good times while we lived in Mineola, after I started my job. We would get off work and head to Lake Lydia and play with Clara and Jerry. Of course, I could write a whole book on the fun times we had with Clara and Jerry. We would swim in the lake and play 42.

One night we were playing 42 and J.D. convinced Clara and Jerry that I had a glass eye. Clara was floored because she had known me for many years and never knew I had a glass eye. J.D. would even touch my eye to convince them and I knew better than to blink or I would have been in trouble.

And then Jerry bought a boat and we would water ski on the weekends; after working on moving the TV antennae, which was a frequent occurrence. Of course the boat Jerry bought would not pull J.D. out of the water, so we would all have to run to the front of the boat to ever get him out of the water. Clara and Jerry always had fun things to do.

We would often go to the Rio Palms Isle in Longview dancing with them and other friends of theirs. They were all older than us and didn't have a problem getting in, but then there was me and J.D. Luckily, or unluckily,

J.D. had a fake ID and we went as Mr. and Mrs. James Attaway. I have no idea where he got this, but it worked. J.D. always insisted on driving, and this was sometimes not good. However, he would always get us home in one piece. We had many good times there, but there were many times that were not so good. When J.D. was drinking too much, he would always get mad even if someone looked at me, and it was really bad if someone, other than the couples we were with, asked me to dance. However, he would agree that we could do the "John Paul Jones." For you who do not know about the John Paul Jones, this is where you changed partners when the whistle was blown. One time I ended up with a really tall man and my feet never touched the floor until the whistle blew and we changed partners. J.D. and I even won a twisting contest at the Rio Palms Isle. He was exceeding happy about that and then decided maybe he was another Fred Astaire, so we had to show out the rest of the night; much to my dismay because I was very shy.

If I ever put on clothes that J.D. did not like, he would tell me I looked like Lula Bell Overstreet. I have no idea who this was, but I knew it was not good, so would try to find something to change into. My wardrobe was pretty limited because you know when you sleep until noon and then watch TV and eat, you have a tendency to put on weight making your clothes shrink.

We would go to parties on the weekend with Jerry and Clara at friends' houses and these were always a lot of fun.

We went to one party at a cabin in the woods and all they had was an outhouse with linoleum around the holes. I was so short that I sat on the hole and when I peed the pee ran down the linoleum into my pants. Clara and I had a good laugh about it, but I had to take my panties off and we threw them in the back of the pickup and I went without panties the rest of the night. When we got home and I got my wet panties out of the back of the pickup, J.D. was drunk, of course, and got really mad because he thought the worst and I was in trouble again. I guess I should have thrown them away, but I didn't have very many pair and decided I had better keep them.

We went on many "free" vacations with them from drawings at the Sports Show in Dallas. All we had to do was look at some property, and the rest of the time was spent having fun. We would go to the Sports Show in Dallas every year and drool over the motor homes and boats and sign up for the free trips.

We even went on a trip to Colorado that was not free. We all loaded up in our little Volkswagen bug and started out. J.D. always wanted to go from Point A to Point B without stopping and this little car got really good gas mileage, so we loaded the cooler with drinks and food and luggage and started off. Clara never slept when we were riding, so Jerry and I would sleep in the backseat while Clara rode up front with J.D. It was really late at night and all of a sudden J.D. came to an abrupt stop and threw Jerry and I both in the floorboard. When we raised up to see what was going on only to find out J.D. had stopped at a red light that was out in the middle of nowhere. As usual, we had a great time on this trip and J.D. was so happy when we started up Pike's Peak and passed all the cars that were pulled over because of overheating. We would rent only one room at the motel and all stay in the same room, which caused many laughs during the night, which I will not go into detail about.

In later years, we would go to Ruidoso, New Mexico to the horse races and spend several days. I would usually have $50.00 to eat on and bet at the track, but that didn't matter when you were betting $2.00 a race for the horses to show, so would end up winning maybe eighty cents a race. I would get just as excited over the eighty cents as the people who were winning a lot more. People would often ask Clara if I had won big and she would have to tell them no; only eighty cents. Also, I loved the Jockeys. I thought they were so cute, especially Jerry Nicodemus. There are not many people in the world that had as much fun as we did, even though we didn't have any money.

Out of my $50.00, I splurged and bought a ham sandwich on rye bread. Of course, J.D. asked for a bite of my sandwich and his bite consisted of half my sandwich. He was using his money to buy beer. At the end of the races, we would have to ride with him, which wasn't too much fun. I yelled at him once when it looked like he was going to hit a car door that was opened into our lane of traffic and he threatened to run me up a telephone pole. I think it even scared Clara and Jerry because they didn't want to be in the car while he was running me up the telephone pole.

Sometimes we would go in Jerry's van and we could sleep in the back. The only problem was it was hot and you would stick to the leather seat and when you tried to roll over it was like pulling Velcro apart.

While living in Mineola, one of J.D.'s school mates, Neil Carter, started to work at the Highway Department and he and his wife, Linda, who was from Winnsboro, lived just a few blocks from us. This was nice to have someone you knew living nearby. I wanted to mention them because it prefaces another funny story about J.D. They invited us to dinner one night and while I was in the kitchen helping her fry chicken, she was going to throw the "knob," you know, the last part to go over the fence, away. I told her not to throw it away because it was J.D.'s favorite piece of chicken. While eating, she noticed that J.D. never picked that piece and pointed it out to him and told him that she fried it especially for him because I told her it was his favorite piece of chicken. This did not go over very well, and you know who ended up in trouble. They had a little redheaded boy named Darwin that was as cute as could be, but he was a real brat. J.D. always said if he had a kid that acted like him, he would kill him. They would come to visit us and he would get on our coffee table and dance and they thought it was so cute. Of course, we did not find it to be so cute because this was our furniture and we tried to take care of it.

After the little sweet couple next door moved out, an older man with his very young bride moved in. He was a character and would bang on our bedroom wall at night when they were going to bed to tell us goodnight. Their bedroom was right next to ours as the duplexes were exactly the same on both sides. He would then bang on the wall to wake us up in the morning. He really was crazy about J.D. and I and hated to see us move.

As I said earlier, we were off to Winnsboro every weekend. Our first winter in Mineola, we left for the weekend and it came a hard freeze. We knew nothing about preparing for a freeze and all we had to heat the house was space heaters in the living room and bathroom. Of course before leaving home we turned all the heaters off and left for the weekend. When we came home our lavatory was just hanging on the wall and all the pipes had frozen and burst. We thought we were doomed, but the man and woman who owned the duplex, Mr. and Mrs. Laminack, were very nice about it and just repaired them. Lord knows, we didn't have the money for repairs.

In 1964, we left Mineola and moved to Dallas for J.D. to go to work at Geo. J. Fix Company as an inside salesman. I think his Uncle Clarence landed this job for him because his uncle and George Fix were friends, as well as Uncle Clarence was a good customer of the Geo. J. Fix Company. This was when the "good times" began. We moved to Pat Drive in Dallas. We still had the chow named Mitsy and our neighbors would not get out of the car if she was in the front yard; we learned many years later. Barbara and Jim Davis were our neighbors, and later our good friends. We only had one decent car, a white Ford Falcon and J.D. bought a clunker with no headlights to drive to and from work. The advantage to this was that he had to be home by dark. Too bad we didn't keep that car. He later traded it for a two-seater Triumph Convertible and hard top. We had a lot of fun in this little car with the top down sporting around.

After we moved to Dallas, we did not know too many people and spent a lot of time with Uncle Clarence and Aunt Neta. We would even go over and babysit for them if they went out on a special occasion. They had two sons, Bobby and Ricky and we loved to keep them. They both thought their Uncle J.D., as they called him, hung the moon. They lived over near White Rock Lake in what I thought was a mansion. It was a very nice, big house and I thought it was just beautiful.

Of course, after we moved to Dallas, I had to search for another job and went through an employment agency. They sent me all over Dallas and even into Irving. I was so shy that interviewing was very difficult for me.

I went on one interview Downtown Dallas at an insurance agency and left there and did not realize I was on a one lane, two way street, which I thought was a one way street. I saw all of these cars lined up ahead of me and I thought they were all parallel parked, so I went around them on the left and noticed when I stopped at a red light facing another car coming at me that all of these cars that I thought were parked actually had people in them. At this point, the only thing I knew to do was back up and get in line before the light changed. This was a bit embarrassing, but I survived it.

I then went on a job interview at State Farm Regional Office on Preston Road and was hired. I was so excited and decided I would go back by Neta's house and tell her about it. I got on Plano Road, which is the road I needed to be on to go to her house. Unfortunately, I went the wrong way on Plano Road and drove and drove and drove until I was out in the country and noticed the road ended and up ahead was just a stretch of dirt road. On up the road, I could see where the road picked up again, so I decided I could just drive on the dirt part and then get back onto the paved road. It had been raining a lot and not being used to black dirt and how sticky it was, I drove for a little bit and stopped and could not get started back, so I just kept trying and ended up sliding off the road into a ditch. At this point, I could see a farmhouse off the road up ahead, so I got out of the car and started walking. I was carrying my footprints with me because every step I took, the black mud stuck to my high heel shoes. I then decided to take my shoes off and carry them because they were so heavy and I walked in my stockings. I really had big feet by the time I got to the gate to the farmhouse. At this time, I noticed a sign on the gate that said "No Trespassing," so I turned around and headed back toward the car and walked the other direction because I could see a pickup beside the road up ahead. There was nobody in the pickup, but then "Zacheus" yelled down from a tree and asked if I needed help. I told him I was stuck and showed him where my car was in the ditch. I told him where I was trying to go and he quickly informed me that I was going the wrong direction. He had a chain in the back of his pickup and took the chain and hooked it onto my car, but could not pull it out and in the process of trying, blew out a tire on his pickup. He then decided that he could get into the car and try to drive it out and told me to get in the back and push, which I did. Every time the car would move a little, I would fall flat on my face. After working and working, we finally got the car out and he told me which way to go and I headed home. This was a couple of hours, at least, that we spent getting the car out, so I decided to go on home and clean me and the car up before I had to go and pick J.D. up at work. I washed the car with a garden hose and got all of the mud off of it and cleaned myself up and did not intend to tell J.D. about my venture. However, on the way home from picking him up, we were on R. L. Thornton Freeway and it sounded like somebody was shooting at us. There were huge chunks of black mud coming from underneath the car onto the freeway. Of course, J.D. said, "God Damn" where is that mud coming from and I had to tell him what had happened. He was not too happy with me, but was not too surprised either. Luckily, I at least had good news for him that I had gotten the job at State Farm. I started to work as a draft typist for the Claims Department and thought I had a very prestigious job. I was very proud of it and was making more money than I had ever made in my life.

Before I started work at State Farm I had no clothes to wear to work because I had outgrown all the dressy clothes I owned and had been wearing uniforms while working at Piggly Wiggly. Lord knows, we did not have money for me to buy clothes, so I went to a cheap dress shop at Big Town; I think it was Lerner's and bought some cheap clothes and a pair of while high heels. It wasn't long before I was walking through the office going to Accounting when the heel popped off of one of my shoes, so I had to spend the rest of the day with a shoe with no heel.

After working at State Farm and living with J.D., I was beginning to not be quite so shy. However, I did have a bad problem of things coming out my mouth before they passed through my brain. For instance, I told the girls at the break table that I hated going for a physical because the nurse always stuck my hole full of fingers. I never realized that I had said anything wrong until everybody died laughing and told me what I had said wrong. Eventually I said so many things wrong unintentionally that one of the girls had me a plaque made of a big mouth with teeth and a tennis shoe sticking in it.

While working at the State Farm Regional Office, one of my friends who was really into witchcraft invited several of us to her house for a reading.

The man who was doing this would have us sit behind a light bulb and he would tell us what he saw. When it came my turn, he looked at me for a long time and then he said he saw a man with a green toolbox standing behind me. This was really weird because my daddy had just died and he always carried a green toolbox with us wherever we went. From this time forward whenever I had car trouble it was always at a place where there was instant help. I do not believe in witchcraft, but I do believe that I have several guardian angels that watch over me; one being my daddy with the green toolbox.

My sister can verify this because she has been with me many times when I had car trouble. One time we were on our way to Winnsboro to Dave's family reunion in our little blue Buick when it overheated at Pickton. A really nice, but strange man offered to drive us on to Winnsboro. My sister rode in the front seat with him and Gena and Ralph, the dog, and I loaded up in the backseat. My sister had a cough and all the way to Winnsboro, he was trying to get her to take a bite of some Vick's that he had in the car.

After getting the little blue Buick fixed, my sister, Gena and I were on our way back from Winnsboro and my sister needed to stop in Greenville to go to the bathroom. When we came out, the car would not start. The men at the station jumped us off and we made it to the other side of Greenville when the windshield wipers stopped working. It was pouring down rain and we knew that we could not stop on the side of Interstate 30 because the car would not start again, so she hung her head out the window and guided me to the next exit so we could get on the service road. After getting on the service road, we could see a station ahead, so we kept creeping along until we arrived at the station. Sure enough, this time the alternator had gone out.

I know this is kind of out of order, but had to share these little stories about my car adventures.

While living on Pat Drive, Jerry and Clara came up to spend the weekend with us and we were going to see Chris Colt and her 45's at a club downtown. We started out in the little while Falcon with J.D. and Jerry in the front seat drinking beer and Clara and I in the backseat. A Corvette pulled out in front of us and J.D. hit it in the side. He and Jerry quickly handed the beer to me and Clara and Clara put it in her purse because we knew the police would be coming. Our car was still driveable so after the accident investigation we were off to see Chris Colt. (I think it was a strip joint, which I had never been to before, and haven't been to since.) Needless to say, J.D. and Jerry enjoyed it and Clara and I were getting to go out so we didn't care.

As I said earlier, they would come up on the weekends and we would always go to the Sports Show to sign up for our free trips.

On one of our free trips, we were on the way to Arkansas with J.D. driving and Jerry in the front seat. We had packed food to take and decided in Texarkana that we would have some bean dip and chips. While opening the bean dip, I cut my finger and had a Kleenex wrapped around it because it was bleeding. I then decided to smoke a cigarette and while lighting it, caught the Kleenex on fire and had to hang my hand out the window with the Kleenex blazing in downtown Texarkana. When Clara would light a cigarette and drop it and we would be scrambling for it,. J. D. and Jerry would always say if there was anything they hated, it was amateur smokers.

After living for a few months on Pat Drive in Dallas, we met our neighbors, Jim and Barbara Davis. They later told us why they were not very friendly. Barbara said she would come home and refused to get out of the car because of our dog, Mitsy. They also told us how they were so worried when we moved in because our moving van was Daddy's red truck with a tarp over the furniture and all they saw was the black man that J.D. had recruited from work to help us unload. We really thought they were just snobs. We later became good friends. They moved to Mesquite and lived on Whit Drive. While visiting them, we found a house that we could afford, and moved just down the street from them. She was a real cute blonde, and J.D. loved to pick on her. They had a little boy named Randy that was adorable. He could never pronounce my name, and called me "Caronon." While living on Whit Drive, they had another son named Brad. After Brad was born, Barbara declared that he was "the end." We would go out partying with them and had a lot of fun.

While J.D. was working at Geo. J. Fix, we also met Larry "Pete" and Dorothy Petersen. J.D. worked with Pete and he invited us to dinner one night to meet his family. While at the dinner table eating roast beef, I was going to say that if there was anything I did not like, it was liver, but instead I said, "If there is anything I do not like, it is roast beef." Needless to say, I did not even realize I had said it wrong until everybody started laughing and J.D. got onto me for saying it. I then had a hard time convincing everybody that I meant to say liver. Pete and Dorothy had three sons, Larry, Michael, and Lee and we fell in love with them right away. Larry was playing little league baseball at the time and we loved going to his games. Michael was very small at the time and was the cutest little redheaded boy that always smiled. Needless to say, we also fell in love with him even though he was a little rotten. Lee had not started to school and was just learning to read Dr. Seuss books. He would climb onto J.D.'s lap and read to us and we both got such a kick out of it. We thought he was about the smartest little boy we had ever known because he could read those books without missing a word.

We were invited to many parties at their house and always had a great time. We would play charades and laughed a lot. They always had fun games to play that did not involve cards or dominoes or board games. It was just good clean fun!!! We attended our first hockey game with them and were so impressed because they knew all the players. I think they had season tickets, but we only went a few times because it was quite expensive.

This began a lasting friendship and I thought they were about the nicest people I had ever met and were always so much fun.

However, things did not stay good for me because J.D. and Pete started going out after work and staying until wee hours of the morning. I was just not used to that and did not like it at all. They said they were shooting pool and Pete told Dorothy where they would go. One night she hired a babysitter and we decided to hunt them down and make sure they were just shooting pool. We parked across the street from the "It'll Do Club" and waited for them to come out so we could follow them. Once again, not such a good idea. As we were sitting there, we saw Pete come out and start walking up the sidewalk headed to a little store to buy cigarettes. He spotted us and headed back to the club and I guess told J.D. and before long here they come in our little blue Volkswagen bug with a mad look on their faces. We were busted and even though Dorothy did not get into trouble, I did. J.D. was so very mad at me and really gave me hell over this. Another big fight was brewing and I knew that I had better hang low and just keep my mouth shut. I always knew "when to hold em and when to fold em" and this was a time I had to fold em. He made me feel like I was the one that was doing something dreadfully wrong. I guess I was in the wrong, but did not realize it. It was a really bad part of town and I'm sure he was concerned that we were even down there. This was the last search party that she and I went on.

Clara and Jerry would come up and visit and we would go to Panther Hall or the Longhorn Ballroom dancing. They came up and went with us to a company Christmas Party at a really nice motel; I think it was the Marriott on Northwest Highway. Mother had made me a red velveteen suit to wear and I really felt dressed up. Before the night was over, everybody started calling me Santa Claus in my red suit and then I was very embarrassed. As I mentioned earlier, I was still very shy and was embarrassed easily.

While J.D. was working with Pete and staying out almost every night; later Pete was coming home but not J.D. After several months, I guess Pete and Dorothy were quite upset with J.D. and decided to tell me he was having an affair with a married girl from the office. I was so upset because I would have bet my life on the fact that J.D. would never run around on me. He always thought it was the worst thing a man could do because that was why his mother and dad had ended up divorced and he knew how hurt his mother was.

The next morning I woke J.D. up and asked him if he had fun with the girl last night. He had the look of a deer caught in the headlights but did not deny it. He asked me how I knew. I asked him if he loved her and he said he did. At this time I felt my heart break right into, literally. However, I went on to work and tried to do my job. This was only the beginning of many heartbreaks.

I later moved into an efficiency apartment on Kingsley in Garland with my friend, Janis Hutchings. She was kind enough to let me live with her for near nothing. We had very close quarters and would go to bed at night on our little sofas and laugh until we eventually went to sleep. Her brother-in-law, Steve Hutchings would come over and we would all go bowling. He was really very entertaining.

J. D. then apologized and talked me into coming back. We did get back together, although things were still not right because I knew I had lost my trust in him, as well as I was still trying to heal from a broken heart.

It was not too long after we got back together that he was about to be drafted into the Army because of the Vietnam war so he enlisted in the Marines. While he was away, I found a girl from Mineola that was on our softball team when we lived there that wanted to move to Dallas and needed a place to stay. I was so happy because I really needed the company as well as the money in order to stay in the house. After she moved in with me, she started showing me all of the scars on her wrist where she had attempted to commit suicide, which was very frightening.

She failed to tell me that she had epilepsy and had seizures. Shortly after she moved in with me, one night around midnight someone started banging on our front door. She peeped out the bedroom window and said it was a black man. We were so scared and the only way to get to the phone which was in the kitchen was to go past the back glass sliding door and I was so afraid I would be seen, but eventually I did run for the phone and called Barbara Davis up the street and asked her to call the police. By this time, it sounded like someone was using a crowbar to try and break in the front door, so we went to the bedroom closet where the guns were and hidden. When the police arrived, I went to the front door with a gun in my hand and when he identified himself, I opened the door with the gun pointed right at him, which scared him. He then went around the house and found "Pete," who told him that he was just there to check on me. Then I went back to the bedroom to get the other girl and she was passed out on the bedroom floor. She had had a seizure. I asked the police officer not to take Pete in because he was a friend, but he took him anyhow. She and I loaded up and went to spend the night with Dorothy, Pete's wife. She had to go the next morning and get him out of jail and I felt so bad.

After the girl could not find a job, she moved back to Mineola, which I was happy about. Barbara Davis, our neighbor and friend, worked with a girl that was looking for a place to live and this girl then moved in with me. I enjoyed her, but did not much enjoy her boyfriend that was there most of the time. He would even spend the night with her, which was something very new to me. I was not raised to think it was okay to spend the night with a man unless you were married to him. She was a very nice girl and helped me out a lot. However, my perfect little world had just gone to pot at this time.

I went to work out at night just to get away and then left town and went to Winnsboro every weekend. For the first time in my life, I was just so mixed up and unhappy. For an early Christmas present, Mother and Mrs. Price gave me the money to fly to San Diego and spend Thanksgiving with J. D. We had Thanksgiving lunch at the hotel dining room, which was quite different than what we were used to. We had a good time, but could not afford to do much but just get out and walk around. I then came back home and spent Christmas with Mother and Daddy and Mr. and Mrs. Price. A few months later, J.D. was released from the Marines with a medical discharge because of the problems with his knee that he had had surgery on years before. He would have been sent to Vietnam otherwise.

I was so proud when I picked him up at the airport because I had lost weight and thought he would be happy, but the first thing he said when he saw me was "God Damn, girl, what has happened to you." This just crushed me. I was so happy to have him back home, but the happiness did not last long.

J.D. went back to work and started not coming home again. After a few months I found out why he was not coming home and we separated again. This time I moved into an apartment on Gaston Avenue with my previous roommate, Ruth. She was living with another girl, Vivian, but let me come and live with them and sleep on the sofa.

All the time I was living there, J.D. was stalking me. He would come over almost every day and knock on the door, but we would not go to the door. This went on for quite a while and then after he promised that he had changed, I went back to live with him. Things were good for a while but soon turned South again and I left one more time.

By this time, Ruth and Vivian had moved to Cedar Springs into an apartment complex that had a private club. I was once again on the soda, but my saving grace was the club where there was dancing every night. I was happy once again because I was dancing and having a good time.

Once again, J.D. was after me to come back to him, so I decided to try it one more time because I loved him so much. This time things were good. He bought me a little black poodle that was so tiny that he could put him in his pocket and walk around. His name was Rebel and he was the cutest ever. The only problem with him was that he would walk under the sofa and come out white because of all the dust. He was also very destructive while we were away at work. He unraveled the carpet between the bedroom and hallway and we had to get this repaired and then he started eating tile on the den floor. But he was still my baby and I always defended him. I was happy once again because I always had something to go home to.

Chapter 5

In December, 1967, the best thing ever happened to me and nine months later, September 17, 1968, the most wonderful gift God has given me was born. I will have to share some of my stories about being pregnant.

To begin with, I was going to a doctor named Dr. Dykes in Oak Cliff. For my first few visits, I always had gained 2 pounds. He sat me down and told me that if I continued gaining 2 pounds every visit, I would be in real trouble. After the lecture he gave me, I stopped eating any bread and always had my bologna on lettuce. This was good because all the time I was pregnant I only gained a total of 14 pounds. I was so lucky because tent dresses were in style at the time and it was difficult to tell I was even pregnant. My cousin, Cheryl, had a lot of these dresses and gave them to me.

My only craving for the nine months was for cement. We were on our way home from work and there was a construction site where they were pouring cement and I smelled it and started craving it. Needless to say, I never ate any, but it didn't keep me from wanting it. My only other desire was for Mexican Food, which we ate every Friday night at the Lakewood El Chico. This is where I had my first Mexican food. I learned many years later, after Pete and I were married, that this is where he and Dorothy ate their first Mexican food. (just a tidbit of information.) All the time I was pregnant, I was so sure in my mind that I was having a boy and the doctor would always tell me I had a 50/50 chance of having a boy. This is before they had such a thing as a sonogram and it was all guesswork.

On the weekend before Gena was born, Pete and Dorothy had a baby shower at their house for all of the Geo. J. Fix employees as well as some of our partying friends. We danced and played games and had a wonderful time. I woke up on Monday morning, September 16th with what I thought was labor pains and J.D. called the doctor to find out it was only contractions. This was good because September 16th was Jerry Ziegler's birthday and he always said if the baby was born on his birthday, he would pay the baby's college tuition. Our good friends, Sherwin and Betty Lou Yokum's baby was also due on the 16th and Jerry promised the same to them. By the way, their baby boy, Brad was born on the 16th

J.D. went on to work and I had these pains all day long and was scared to death. He and Mother were calling continuously all day long and every time I would get comfortable, the phone would ring and I would have to go from the bedroom to the kitchen and have to lie down in the hallway on the way to the phone because the pain was so severe. The doctor then told J.D. to take me on to the hospital and they said it was only contractions and sent me back home. The doctor told J.D. to bring me to his office the next morning and he would check me. The contractions continued all through the night and on the way to the doctor's office in the car. We finally arrived and the doctor gave me a shot and told J.D. to take me to the hospital emergency entrance. After circling Methodist Hospital what felt like 3 times, we finally found the Emergency entrance and I was wheeled into the labor room and this is when the fun started. Gena finally arrived at 8:10 p.m. When I woke up the first person I saw was my mother and I said "Hi, Mommy," which I never called her Mommy. By the time I left the recovery room, it was very late and I was taken to my room and was not allowed to see my baby. However, before J.D. left to go home, he told me it was a little girl with a head full of black hair.

The next morning the nurse brought me a baby with no hair and I refused to take her. I told the nurse my husband told me my little girl had a head full of black hair, so this must be the wrong baby. While they were checking on this, J.D. arrived and I found out it really was my baby. To come to find out, when he saw her, her head was badly bruised from the forceps they had to use and it looked like a head full of black hair. J.D.

never mentioned it to me, but he was so worried because instead of being round, her head was kind of pointed due to the use of forceps. He quickly found the doctor and the doctor told him that it would not be pointed for long. To me, she was just perfect. I was so in love from the moment I found out she was mine. I was happy it was a girl even though I could hardly believe it. We then had to decide on a name. We had several boy names picked out, but had decided on Gena Kay for the girl. J.D. added the "e" to Kay, which was fine with me. The Kay was after my cousin, Cheryl Kay. J.D. and I both loved the name "Gina," which was close to the name of one of our favorite people in the world, Tina, but since our baby girl was so unique, we felt she needed a different spelling of her name. Therefore, we named her Gena with an "e" instead of an "i". I was in the hospital until Friday and was in the room with a girl that had just had a 10 pound boy, which was her third. Here I was on Cloud 9 and she would just lie in the bed and moan and groan and did not seem too interested in anything but her pain. I was about the happiest person in the world and had no pain. The only time I unwrapped Gena was to dress her to come home from the hospital and that was a real experience. I had no clue how to change a diaper or dress a crying baby. I was literally scared to death, but with J.D.'s help, we managed to get her dressed and started our trip home.

We lived on Whit Drive in Mesquite in a house with only one little window unit air conditioner when Gena was born. Mother and Dorothy were at the house sterilizing everything in the house when we arrived home. J.D. said he figured he would be the next thing to go in the boiling water. Thanks to Mother and Mrs. Price, we had a fully equipped nursery. Most everything in the nursery was purchased with Mother and Mrs. Price's S&H Green Stamps. I had so much fun shopping with them. Since Barbara Davis had declared that she would have no more babies, she gave me her little chest and mother painted it white, along with the used baby bed that she had bought for Gena. Mother stayed for two weeks and helped me with learning to take care of a baby. When she left to go home, she told me the most important thing was to make sure and keep her warm. I put a heavy gown on her and wrapped her up in a flannel blanket, turned the small air conditioner off and put her in the bassinette.

As I mentioned earlier, it was September and very hot outside, but my goal was to keep her warm. It wasn't long until she started crying and cried all day long, with Rebel the dog sitting looking at me as if to say, please do something to make that baby stop crying. When J.D. got home from work, Gena was crying, I was crying and Rebel was upset too. He called Barbara Davis up the street and asked her to please come and help because he didn't know what to do. In the meantime, before Barbara arrived, he was on the phone calling Mother and begging her to please come back. When Barbara came in the house and found Gena in a heavy gown wrapped up in a flannel blanket in the hot house, she quickly detected the problem. She took Gena out of the bassinette and unwrapped her and took the heavy gown off her and she immediately stopped crying. Of course, by this time Mother was on the way. When she arrived, everything was okay. Mind you, I was just following orders and keeping the baby warm.

After Mother left, I never took my eyes off of Gena. I pulled the bassinette behind me everywhere I went. If I went outside to hang up clothes, because we did not have a clothes dryer, the bassinette was right behind me. She slept in the bassinette right beside our bed with my hand on her all night long. I never left the house for 6 weeks and then we had to go for her first checkup.

In the meantime, J.D. was transferred to Longview to work for the Geo. J. Fix office in Longview, so this meant we had to move when Gena was 6 weeks old. We rented a house in Longview and we would take Gena to Mother's to stay while we were getting the house ready to move in. Clara helped out tremendously. This house had more cabinets than you can imagine, and we had to clean all of the cabinets and put down shelf paper. Clara and J.D. painted the nursery. I was not such a good painter, so they would not let me help.

We packed and moved in one day, with J.D. and his recruits loading the truck and moving, leaving me behind to clean the house on Whit Drive. It took me hours to clean, and then I drove to Longview. Shortly after arriving in Longview, we had a phone call from Daddy begging us to please come and get Gena because Mother was a wreck. We loaded up and drove to Winnsboro to pick her up and then back to Longview to unpack.

The next week Gena and I stayed in bed all day long except to feed her and do laundry. I hurt all over, from head to toe, and was just about past going.

At the time, I was on maternity leave from State Farm. When my maternity leave expired, I had to start looking for a job, but was lucky when I found out that the State Farm office had two secretaries; one had been there for 5 years and the other 10 years. I felt pretty safe because I found out from the employment agency that I did not have to take a job making less than I was making at State Farm, so I started drawing unemployment. This was too good to be true because in Longview there were no secretarial jobs that paid as much as State Farm in Dallas.

Gena and I would load up in the little Volkswagen bug, with her in her little carrier laying in the right front passenger seat and go to Winnsboro to spend the day. We never owned a car seat. When she got too big for her carrier, she would just sit in the right front passenger seat. There was no such things as seat belts, and yes, she survived.

Then my luck ran out when I had a call from State Farm that the girl in the office that had been there for 10 years was leaving and I could have the job. Gena was then 6 months old and we had to start looking for a babysitter. We were lucky to find a lady, Mrs. Davis, that would come to the house and stay with her. She did nothing but hold Gena all day long and watch television, which was fine with me. I would rush home to check on her during my lunch hour, and always found her holding Gena and rocking her. We just loved her, but a few weeks after she kept Gena, she told us that she could no longer keep her, so we had to start looking for another babysitter. This is just another example of how God always watches over us because within two weeks after she quit babysitting, she died with a heart attack. We found another girl that would keep Gena that was crippled and not much bigger than Gena, but we hired her because she seemed to be okay.

I loved my job at State Farm and worked with a girl named Mary Lou. We shortly became good friends. While working there, she married Floyd Pepper and Floyd and J.D. hit it off too, so we had friends to go out to eat with. Fortunately, they loved Mexican food also and we would go to El Chico's. They loved Gena too. She was never any trouble to take out because she would just sit in her little carrier and watch us eat.

After I started back to work, we decided to buy a house and found a cute little house on Baxley Lane in Longview. It was just perfect to me and so here we were moving again. It was a beautiful neighborhood and we shortly met the couple that lived across the creek from us, Sharon and Danny Rushton. They did not have children, and quickly fell in love with Gena. We had a wooded area behind our house with lots of trees. We just loved it there. Sharon and I would walk Gena every day after work in her stroller.

While living in Longview, we came to Dallas to yet another Geo. J. Fix Christmas party. This time Mother made me a really cute while fringe dress to wear. Pete and Dorothy had asked us to come and stay with them and after we started getting ready to go to the party, I discovered that I did not bring any panty hose. I was going to go and buy some, but Dorothy said she had a pair I could wear. They were black and looked really good with my white fringe dress. However, when we arrived at the Christmas party and got on the elevator to go to the floor where the party was, I looked down and the black panty hose were twisted around on both legs, which was not very attractive. Oh well, we were going to have fun despite the twisted black panty hose.

We were having a great time and I thought all was well. One of the black men that J.D. worked with asked me to dance and since J.D. worked with him, I thought the only thing to do was dance with him. Needless to say, this started World War III. When I got back to my seat, J.D. was furious and of course, Pete just egged it on. J.D. was mad over this the rest of the weekend and refused to have anything to do with me because I danced with a black man. It took forever and a day for him to get over this, and of course, Pete was not helping any. Just another time I was in trouble for being innocent and doing what I thought was the right thing.

This is another funny little story about J.D. while we were living in Longview. He volunteered to keep Gena one day while I went to the beauty shop. While I was gone, he was having so much fun watching her in her bassinette turning red in the face. Since he did not keep her often, he didn't really know what to expect. He then began to smell something, and sure enough, this meant she was having bowel trouble and had literally filled her diaper. He ended up having to put her in the lavatory to clean her up and had to change the sheets on the bed where he was changing her. I don't think he ever volunteered to keep her by himself again until we moved back to Dallas, which is another story.

Gena spent her first Christmas in Longview. J.D. and Jerry volunteered to keep her one evening while Clara and went to Tyler to do our Christmas shopping. We always shopped well together because I would say, do you think so-and-so would like this and she would always say yes, and it was purchased. We always had lots of laughs but we always helped each other out and could complete our Christmas shopping in one night. Clara and Jerry did not have any children and really did not plan on having any. However, Gena changed their mind. They decided that they should maybe consider having a baby. About 2 years later, Laura Jane was born.

Two weeks before Gena turned one, J.D. came home from work and informed me that we were moving back to Dallas. He was going to leave Geo. J. Fix and go to work for Briggs Weaver. His uncle Clarence had gotten him the job and he was pretty excited about it. I was not excited at all.

The day Gena turned one we were moving to Garland. She celebrated her first birthday with a little party at Mamaw's house. We were then off to Garland to Pleasant Valley. We had bought a cute little house that we could not afford on Pleasant Valley in Garland where we would start another phase of our life.

Chapter 6

J.D. started his job with Briggs Weaver and I transferred back to State Farm. At the time, they did not have any openings for claims secretaries, so I went to work as a Service Correspondent, which meant that I handled phone calls from agents and customers and tried to resolve problems on files over the phone.

Since I did not have a babysitter, I had to leave Gena at a day care facility, which was very difficult for me to do. The days were extremely long and when I would pick her up, she always smelled bad. Even though I was sending clothes for them to change her, they would just clean her up and put the same dirty clothes back on her. She was sick almost every day, I think because she did not like being left there.

After several weeks, I could not bear it any longer and Mother and Mrs. Price came up and stayed with her while I was searching for a babysitter. While they were staying with her, they had to trick her into eating; one would do tricks while the other fed her. I came home from work one day and they were both exhausted. To come to find out, the bedroom where they were staying was infested with tics. This was because when we lived in Longview, I had a box of my treasures stored under our bed where Rebel always slept. As I mentioned earlier, we lived in a wooded area in Longview and I guess Rebel was getting tics when we let him out in the backyard and then he would bring them in and sleep under the bed. Anyway, this box of treasures was full of tics and they had made their way out of the box and the whole wall in the spare bedroom was covered in tics. They had been killing tics all day long by bleaching the walls in the bedroom. Thank goodness, there was no carpet in the spare bedroom at the time and they were able to get them under control.

A girl that worked at State Farm, Bonnie McGhee, told me about a babysitter that she had used for her girls that was just great. I contacted her, Shirley Johnson, and she said she would be happy to keep Gena. She had three children of her own, Cara, who was just a couple of years older than Gena, Susan, who was the oldest, Michael and Kevin. This was just perfect and Gena loved staying with her. As a matter of fact, she later called Shirley her daytime Mom. Shirley also kept a couple of other girls, one part-time and the other full time, so Gena loved it. Gena and Cara were almost like sisters years later.

I would take Gena to Shirley's and pick her up on my way home from work. She never was ready to go home. She would always ask if Cara could go home with us.

Our house on Pleasant Valley had a dressing area right outside the bathroom and while Gena was staying with Shirley she told her that her mother and daddy took showers together. I guess she thought since we were both back in our bedroom getting ready that we were in the shower together.

She also told Shirley when she asked Gena what kind of work her daddy did that he made music and drank beer. This was because the only time she had been to his office was for company picnics.

Shortly after we moved back to Garland, a really nice couple, Barbara and Dennis Hall moved next door. They did not have any children and loved Gena. Gena could not say Barbara and called her Barber. Gena thought Barbara was her age and always wanted to go play with Barber. Dennis traveled with his job and Barbara did not like to stay by herself at night, so she would come and spend the night with Gena or Gena would spend the night with her. Barbara would read stories to Gena until she fell asleep. Every time Dennis went out of town, he would always bring something back to Gena, who he called "Gena Bodena." They were great neighbors and we spent a lot of time together.

One day Barbara and I went to Treasure City shopping because she loved to shop and I needed hairspray, "Aqua Net," which Treasure City carried. Barbara had picked up something on the sale table, which was not on sale and was charged full price at the register. She even took them back and showed them the sign where she got it and they would not let her have it for the sale price. She got mad and told them she did not want anything she had in her basket and told them that the girl behind her did not want what she had either. Mind you, I really needed that Aqua Net because I was out, but she proceeded to drag me out of the store without my Aqua Net.

Another little funny story was when Barbara rode with me to the Bank of America to get money one evening and while we were waiting to turn left onto the street to go to the bank, a police officer pulled from a Stop Sign and hit my car. Because it was a police officer, it took a long time to investigate the accident. While we were out talking to the officer, Gena decided to clean out the floorboard in the back of my car, throwing trash out onto the street. Thank goodness, I noticed it before the police officer did and was able to stop her.

Another time, Barbara, Gena and I went to Valley View shopping and when we got into the car to leave, we could not back up. I was parked beside a curb and my front right tire was in front of the curb. We swore they built a curb around my tire while we were shopping.

Barbara and I neither one liked to cook, so we decided we would take turns cooking dinner and eat with each other. Gena was not into eating at this time and would always say her arms were tired is why she did not want to eat and we would take turns feeding her. I always enjoyed eating with them except they had a really nice dining room suite with velveteen chairs and I was always afraid Gena would mess the chairs up, so we would put a towel on the chairs to protect them. Of course, with our feeding her, that was not likely to happen.

Barbara and Dennis had two Dashounds that were like babies and Gena loved playing with them. She could even dress them up like they were babies. Barbara and Dennis had a nice boat, and on the weekends when we did not go to Winnsboro, we were off to Cedar Creek Lake to go water skiing. Gena loved riding in the boat and would just sit there with her life jacket on and ride and sleep while we skiing. We always had a great time and later got us a tent and would camp out at the lake.

We had many great times together and had many laughs. Barbara and Dennis went with us to one of J.D.'s company parties. The tables were decorated with candles and when it was almost over, we told J.D. and Dennis that we needed one of those candles for Gena's jack-o-lantern. Before we knew it, J.D. and Dennis had gathered up all of the table decorations and put them in the cooler to bring them home. Needless to say, before they finished, they were busted and they made them put them all back and we ended up with no candle.

While living on Pleasant Valley, Gena learned to ride a bicycle with J.D. and I taking turns holding onto the seat and running up and down the sidewalk behind her. We lived right across the street from Weaver Elementary School that had a playground and a nice area to ride bicycles and fly kites. However, since we were not home too much during the day because of work and were gone almost every weekend, Gena only had a couple of friends in the neighborhood to play with. She did finally meet a couple of little girls to play with.

When Shirley could not keep Gena, Aunt Syble and Jim would volunteer to keep her. She loved going to Aunt Syble's house because Jim would play with her and Aunt Syble would take her to the park down the street from her to play. She always called it Aunt Syble's park.

While working as a Service Correspondent, because it was often hard to understand names on the phone, I would often ask if that was so-and-so like in so-and-so. One morning I asked if that was "S" like in, and for the life of me, could not think of any word that began with "S" other than "shit." Mind you, it was early and my brain was not working very good. I thought to remedy that happening again, I came up with words that I always used for initials. One morning I had a phone call shortly after arriving at work from a lady that said her name was Mrs. J.N. Smith and

I asked her if that was "N" like in "lucky," and there was a long pause and then she came back with no, that is "N" like in Smith. Thank goodness, she was a good sport and we both just died laughing. What a way to start the day.

One of Carolyn Wallace and Cathy Fowler's favorite stories about me also happened while I was working as a Service Correspondent. I had a phone call and went up to the file cabinets, where they both worked as file clerks, pulled a file out of one of the bottom drawers, raised up and one of the staples caught the hem of my dress and I was walking back to my desk reviewing the file with my dress pulled up and never knew it. They loved this and still talk about it.

While working at the State Farm Regional Office, Bonnie McGhee and I started riding together. Bonnie and Ralph McGhee had three girls, Joanie, Patti and Valarie, and the two older girls, Joanie and Patti, would babysit for us when we went out. While we were riding back and forth to work, Bonnie called everybody an "old Bastard" if they did something wrong. Of course, J.D. used a curse word just about every other word, but Gena never repeated what he said. However, on the way home from Shirley's, a man pulled out and almost hit us and I called him an old Bastard. It wasn't long after that J.D. picked Gena up at Shirley's and on their way home Gena pointed and told him that was where that old bastard almost hit us. Of course, he got a kick out of it and I was busted.

On our way to work one morning, Gena was sitting beside me on the front seat and we were stopped at the red light at five points, i.e., Highway 78, Garland Avenue and First Street and she asked me, "What is a Mamma Fucker." I almost ran the red light when she asked this. I asked her where she had heard that and she told me that Jennifer, another little girl younger than Gena that Shirley kept, called people that. My first reaction was to tell her she was saying it wrong, but I quickly told her that she shouldn't be saying that because it wasn't very nice.

While living on Pleasant Valley, Mary Lou and Floyd came up to spend the weekend with us. We had a pool table in the garage and J. D. and

Floyd were out shooting pool and Mary Lou and I were going shopping. Gena was asleep in her baby bed in her room so we asked J.D. and Floyd to watch her while we were out shopping. We were gone for several hours and then stopped back by the convenience store on the way home and I came out of the store and saw J.D. and Floyd come flying up in J.D.'s little blue Datsun pickup. I went over to the pickup and asked him where Gena was; he said "God Damn" and burned out of there 90 to nothing. They had forgotten that they were watching Gena and had just run to the store to get some cigarettes. Sure enough, she was okay and was just standing in her baby bed talking when we arrived home.

While working at the State Farm Regional Office, on February 25th, 1972, I had just got settled in at work when the State Farm nurse came to my desk and wanted me to come with her. She took me to the sick room and then proceeded to tell me that she had a phone call that my daddy had passed away. Even though I knew he was in Doctor's Hospital on Garland Road in Dallas for tests to be run, this was devastating news. We had been to visit him the evening before and I knew he was really sick, but I had no idea he was about to die. I went into shock and the next few days were like a fog. Mother was staying with Aunt Syble during the day and with us at night while he was in the hospital. We had just celebrated his 69th birthday at my house on February the 18th. with a big party. Aunt Syble had retired and she and Jim had moved to Garland to be close to her brothers. Daddy was loving having her nearby, and they had even been on a couple of trail rides together since she moved back.

I had dreamed many times that my daddy had died and we were at his funeral when I would wake up so happy because it was only a nightmare. All during his funeral, I kept wishing I could wake up and find that he had not died. Gena was only two when Daddy died and then she was about 4 when Mr. Price died. After that, she thought everybody that went into the hospital died, so we had to be very careful to explain to her this was not the case.

Ray and Janie came to Mr. Price's funeral and Janie had on a full length "Black Diamond" fur that was just beautiful. A few weeks later, I took Gena to the nice little children's dress shop in Ridgewood to try and find her a coat. Of course, we didn't have much money, but she found a blue furry coat that she just loved because she said it looked like a "Blue Diamond" fur. This put me between a rock and a hard place because the coat was quite expensive and with my daughter knowing her furs, I didn't want to let the store clerk know we couldn't afford it, so I bought it. I guess it was worth it because she always loved that coat.

After Daddy died, Mother had a very difficult time because she would not stay by herself. Her sister, Eunice, lived with her for a while and after she left, she would go over and spend the night with Aunt Myrtie. We would go down and stay with her on the weekends.

My sister and Roy came down and helped her find a house in town and she moved to town, but this still did not help. The week before Daddy would have been gone a year, she called me one evening and told me she was getting married the next day. I didn't even know she was seeing anyone, rather on getting married. I was so shocked and went into a rampage saying things I should have never said. I think it was because I was in shock. She said she had only had a couple of dates with him, but he was a really nice man and Mr. and Mrs. Dodgen had introduced them. His name was Dave Honeycutt and was a neighbor of theirs. I was truly upset and did not see Mother for a while because she did not need me to come on the weekends.

One weekend she called and wanted to bring Dave to meet us, which was fine. When Gena found out his name was Honeycutt, she wanted to know if she could call him "Honeybee" and that is what she called him, and believe me, he was a Honeybee.

Gena would go down and stay with them and when Mother would take her to the dime store, Perry Brothers, which was daily, she would only let her buy little things. If she found something that was more than Mother would spend, she would go back to the house and ask Dave to take her because he would buy her whatever she wanted.

When my sister and the kids came for the summer, Tina told Gena they should call Dave Grandpa instead of Honeybee and from that time on, he was Grandpa.

Dave was one of the nicest men I have ever known and was truly a blessing to our family. He treated Mother like a princess. He did all of the housework and laundry and would take her to nice places to eat and bought her jewelry and a fur coat. He loved her so much and she was exceedingly happy. They were married for about fourteen years before he died. He loved me and would have done anything in the world for me. I often thought he treated me better than his own children, but I was also good to him and did a lot for him.

After several years, along came Baby Beth. Shortly after Beth was born, we moved from Pleasant Valley to Reinosa Drive; in September 1976.

I was now working for State Farm as a claims adjuster. After being promoted to claims adjuster, I had to attend Claims School in Bloomington, Illinois. This was my first trip away from home alone, and boy, was it an adventure. I will have to elaborate on this because it is a book within itself. I was supposed to fly from D/FW Airport to St. Louis, Missouri on American Airlines and then catch a small plane from St. Louis to Bloomington, with only a short time to change planes. Our flight at D/FW was delayed by about an hour, which meant it would take a miracle for me to catch my plane in St. Louis. When we arrived in St. Louis, the man seated next to me on the plane asked the stewardess if we could get off the plane first to try and catch my connecting flight. He was familiar with the airport and said he could take me right to the gate. She agreed and we were off and running, to no avail. I had already missed my flight. He then took me to the American Airlines desk and told them what my problem was and they told me to go and stand nearby and they would try and find a place for me to stay the night and I could fly out the next morning.

While I was standing waiting, the girl came over and told me there was a group of guys that were going to try and catch the train and for me to go with them. They grabbed my suitcases and off we went to try and catch the train. One of the guys stopped the train and we all loaded on. They did not let me out of their sight the entire trip. I learned in talking to them that they had been to Boys Town in Mexico and were on their way home. They even told me about Boys Town and what they had been doing there, which was a little frightening to me, but, after all, they were watching after me. This was in December and when we arrived in Bloomington, the ground was covered in snow.

As I was getting off the train, one of the engineers asked if anyone needed a ride. The guys quickly said, she does. I told him no; I had money to take a cab. The engineer asked where I was going and insisted that he take me there. He took me to his pickup truck and turned the heater on to defrost the windshield and told me he had to go in the station for a minute, but would be right back. When he got back, we took off bound for my motel and as we went through town, I saw a movie theater that had a sign that said "Fritz the Cat" was showing. I told the engineer that I loved Walt Disney movies and would have to see that. I later found out this was a porn movie at an X-Rated theater. He then dropped me off at my motel, unloaded my luggage, kissed me on the cheek and said he hoped I had a good week. He refused to take any money from me.

I then proceeded to my room where I found my roommate that looked like a lesbian which in those days we called a "Butch." I immediately thought this was going to be a long week. After talking with her, I found out she had recently graduated from college and was a newlywed. This was quite a relief.

I had never seen so much snow in my whole life, and being from the Dallas area, only had a very light jacket with me and high heel shoes and dresses to wear to class. We were supposed to walk to class, which was only a few blocks away. The next morning there was 13 inches of snow and I headed out walking on what I thought was the sidewalk with my high heels and snow up to my "uh-huh." I had only walked about a half a block when one of the guys that was running the snow shovel scooping snow off the street yelled at me to come out and walk in the street.

The classes were quite interesting, and the whole class was from the North, with me being the only southerner in the class. This might have been to my advantage because they were all very young and very smart, and I was as dumb as a stump. However, I think just my opening my mouth was very entertaining to them. I never had the right answer, but I would give the whole class, including the instructor, a good laugh with my answers to questions. I was not making very good grades because we had to take notes in class just like in college and then study our notes. It seems that my problem was that I was taking down unimportant information and missing the important information.

After a few days, my roommate asked if she could help me and after reviewing my notes, determined that I did not know much about taking notes in class. She then let me review her notes, and my grades improved.

When we would go out in the evenings to eat, we would come back and our keyhole would be frozen over and we would have to go to the manager to get him to let us back in the room using a blow torch. We would walk to downtown in the evenings because the square was absolutely beautifully decorated for Christmas with music playing. Even though it was beautiful, it would make me homesick. Overall, I had a great time at claims school and did pass. The instructor wrote a letter to State Farm telling them what a pleasure it was to have me in his class. He told State Farm that even though my grades were not the best, that he thought I would make a very good claims adjuster.

I then began training as a claims adjuster at the Claims Office at LBJ and Audelia Road in the Bodily Injury Claims Department. This was a real experience. Jim Keil was my mentor, and after a week or two of training, I was on my own. After a few months in this department, I transferred to the Property Damage Section and worked with Jean Stanton, Fred Gibson and Jim Wood. This was a job that required a lot of talking on the phone and trying to convince people that the accident was their fault, after taking telephone statements. This was a very difficult job. For one thing, nobody ever felt they were at fault in an accident and if their car was totaled, it was the best car they had ever owned. It was not an easy job for me, but because of the people I worked with being so much fun, I was able to endure it.

One little example of the fun we had at work was when I was handling a claim for a young man who was a junior and I could never tell the difference in his and his father's voices so when one called, I asked if it was the father or the son and Fred Gibson, who sat behind Jean at the back of the office stood up and said real loud "or the holy ghost." I could hardly talk and had to excuse myself for a minute until I could quit laughing. However, this job was changing me in the wrong way because I always loved people and trusted everybody. I lived claims 24 hours a day. I was continuously working claims in my mind. Also, during this time. J.D. was not coming home at night and I was coming home worn out, fixing dinner, and he would not show up.

When Gena started Kindergarten, she went to Centerville Elementary School because that is where Shirley's children went. Her teacher was Mrs. Suiter and Gena loved her. Gena was very smart, but Mrs. Suiter told J. D. and I that we had to lighten up on her because she would not put anything on paper until she checked with the teacher for fear it would be wrong. She was also a rule follower and had a tendency to tell on other kids if they were doing something wrong. In other words, she was a perfectionist.

While attending Centerville Elementary, one of her teachers told us she needed to go to speech therapy. This almost did J.D. in because he knew she did not need speech therapy. He and Billy Bass were about to go to school and jump on this teacher because in their eyes, Gena was perfect and did not need any help with her speech.

Our first family vacation was to Galveston. This was Gena's first time to stay in a motel and she thought it was just the utmost. It was right across the street from the beach, which she did not like too much, except she and her Dad would pick up seashells. She liked doing that, but did not like the water.

Our next vacation was to Disney World and she loved it. J.D. was not too crazy about the long lines that we had to wait in to ride the rides, but tolerated it because Gena was having so much fun. She was so excited all the time we were there. J.D. said he would not come back to Disney World until he had grandchildren so he could push them around in a stroller and run over everybody.

However, we then went back to Disney World when Gena was in high school and Barbara, Dennis and Beth went also. We had a great time, but while we were there, I had a call that one of my best friends, Jean Stanton, had passed away. This was devastating news, but I knew I could do nothing but continue on. This was our very last family vacation.

When Gena was in the 3rd Grade, I left State Farm and started typing for court reporters at home. It was really nice to be able to take her to school and pick her up in the afternoons and spend time with her. This also enabled me to be a room mother. Of course, I had to work many long hours and had to be very disciplined.

During this time our little black poodle, Rebel, passed away with congestive heart failure and J.D. informed me it was his time to get the kind of dog he wanted. He and Gena went to look at a black Lab, which is what he wanted, but came home with a little ball of fur. He found out right quick he could not afford a black Lab, so he came home with a Chow and named him Rusty. He could not even climb the stairs when we got him. He was adorable and we all loved him, but he was definitely J.D.'s dog.

As Rusty grew up, we had to be very careful not to run in the house because he did not like fast movement and would try to attack you. Gena then decided she wanted a dog of her own so she could name him "Ralph." This was because her Dad always called her Ralph and people would think he was talking about the dog instead of her. She wanted a little black poodle just like Rebel. It took me a few years of working on J.D., but he finally agreed we would surprise her one Christmas with her own little black poodle and she was so excited and did name him Ralph.

In September, 1976, we moved into our new home at 640 Reinosa Drive. I had found this house while being lost in the area while it was being built. It was my dream home and I fell in love with it. I told J.D. about it and he said there was no way we could afford it, but I started trying to figure out a way to afford it and finally convinced him that we could do it. Nothing was ever easy for us. The day we were supposed to move in, we went to get the key and found out our loan had not been approved and the utilities had not been turned on. The builder assured us that everything would be okay, but we could not stay in the house until the loan was approved. We continued with the move-in and had to stay at a motel until the loan was approved and the utilities were turned on. What a nightmare.

Shortly after moving in, J.D.'s job changed and he lost his company car and expense account. It looked like we were going to be in big trouble, but once again, God took over.

I typed for court reporters until Gena started high school. I was at home when she was in Middle School at O'Banion, which made it really nice. The only problem was that I was not making much money. J.D. decided when Gena started high school that I needed to get a real job to start saving for college.

After living here a short time, my sister's husband, Roy, died and she and Chad and Tina moved from Pittsburgh, Pennsylvania to Garland and stayed with us until they could find a house. I flew to Pittsburgh to drive she and the kids and their pug, Queenie, back to Texas. Of course these were trying times for her and even she and J.D. seemed to get along in the time they were with us. J.D. was working in outside sales and would come home during the day at different times so she had to be on her toes because when he left in the mornings she would put a sheet over his little table beside his recliner. My sister was not big on clutter and hated the looks of that table that had everything he needed or would ever need on it.

Speaking of their pug, Queenie, I must tell a funny story about J.D. and Queenie. While living in Pittsburgh, my sister and her family and the pug flew down and J.D. picked them up at the airport in our white Mercury. Later in the day he had to take a customer to lunch and the customer had on a dark suit. And if you know anything about pugs, they have blonde hair and shed profusely. Queenie had ridden in the front floorboard of the car and needless to say, had shed all over the floorboard. J.D. did not have time to clean it out before he picked the customer up. When the customer got out of the car, his dark suit was covered with dog hair and he started brushing it off. J.D. just looked at him and said, "God damn, I hope you didn't get that all over my car." He never bothered to tell the customer where the dog hair came from.

After moving back to Texas, my sister and the kids stayed with us until she could find a house to buy and ended up moving only a few blocks from us on Wildbriar. It was nice to have them so close.

One weekend when we all went to Winnsboro, I was going down to Mrs. Price's and Chad wanted to go with me. I asked him if he wanted to drive and he quickly said yes. I assumed he knew how to drive, but quickly learned after making the right turn from Highway 11 to go to Perryville on two wheels that he had never driven a car. He didn't even apply the brakes when we turned. Other than that, he did pretty good.

Gena and I loved having them stay with us because she had company and I had a lot of help. J.D. tolerated them and actually was on his best behavior during this time. My sister took a job at Gena's school as a teacher's aide with the special needs teacher and this really made Gena happy.

Because my sister lived so far away, and we only saw them once a year, I did not have an opportunity to spend much time with her and Chad and Tina, so I was loving having them in Garland, but not loving the circumstance that brought them here. We had many good times together now that they were here, i.e., water skiing trips and camping. Tina started Middle School at O'Banion and Chad started High School at Lakeview. Chad graduated high school and went to North Texas State University. Tina did not go to college, but married John and worked. After Chad finished college, he married Cindy and they lived in Garland.

And then along came my great nieces and nephew, Megan, Chase and Cassie.

I started work for an attorney in Garland named Stuart Pastor and his office was about 5 minutes from home, which meant I could come home for lunch every day. It was an interesting job but did not pay very well. However, I gained some valuable experience. He was exceedingly nice and thought I walked on water. I more or less ran the office and even took statements from witnesses over the phone.

Since I was at home for lunch every day, I decided to teach Ralph to speak for food. We thought it was pretty cute until we would have company and he would stand at the table and keep speaking until someone would feed him. Another big mistake of mine.

The first month I worked there, J.D. came home with a four-wheeler he had bought. I asked him if he bought it for Gena to ride to college. Once again, I had definitely said the wrong thing and he got mad about it.

While working in this office, I had another Carolyn moment. I had borrowed paper from an office down the hallway and was returning it one day when I decided on my way back to the office I would stop by the restroom. From our office, you always went past the water fountain and it was the first door past the water fountain. On my way back to the office, I went past the water fountain and opened the door and lo and behold there was the man in the office next to us standing peeing. I could not believe my eyes. I just stood there and then I said, I'm sorry Mike, which was not even his name. He just died laughing and I went back to my office and tried to figure out what to do; i.e., leave Stuart Pastor a note that I was leaving my job or go down the hallway and apologize. After pondering for a while, I decided I would just go and apologize. When I walked in to apologize, he said he felt he owed me an apology for laughing but he said the look on my face cracked him up. Anyhow, I apologized and went on my way.

I worked there until Gena graduated high school and needless to say, was not able to save much money. During this time, things were not so good with J.D. and I. He seldom came home until the wee hours of the morning and needless to say, I knew he was probably having another affair, but I was not in a situation that I could say anything. I did not make enough money to support myself, rather on send Gena to college. This meant I just had to keep my mouth shut and pretend everything was okay.

Another family vacation was to San Antonio. We stayed right on the river, went to the San Antonio Zoo, rode the River Boat, visited the Brewery and the Alamo and had a great time. On the way to San Antonio, we decided to spend the night in Austin so we could take Gena to see the capitol. I'm pretty sure they put us in a room at the motel that was usually occupied by prostitutes because all night long we had knocking on our door. Finally, J.D. had had enough and sat straight up in the bed and yelled, "What the hell do you want." The knocking stopped and we were able to get a few hours of sleep.

On the way back home, we stopped in New Braunfels and took a raft down the river. Our guide was really nice and stopped at the cliff where people would jump and wanted to know if anyone wanted to join him in jumping off the cliff. I told him I would and we proceeded to climb the cliff. It was a horrible climb up the cliff and after getting to the top, you just knew there was only one way down, and that was to jump. The guide jumped off and I sat down for a few minutes and caught my breath and then walked over and jumped. He never told me that I had to keep my legs and arms straight when I jumped, so the only thing I did was hold my nose. When I jumped, I hit the water so hard that I thought I had knocked my left leg off. I went so far under that by the time I came to the top, J.D. was about to jump in to find me. We found out later they had banned jumping off this cliff because so many people had got killed doing it. It was extremely scary to say the least. I was lucky to only end up with a badly bruised leg.

After Gena left for college, J.D. never came home at night and then informed me that he wanted a divorce. He said he would stay with me until I found a job that paid enough for me to support myself.

I went to work and told Stuart Pastor that I had to find another job unless he could pay me more. He said he could not possibly pay me enough to support myself, but I could take all the time off I needed to find another job.

I found a tiny little ad in the newspaper for a legal secretary at a law firm downtown. I called and set up an interview, bought me a new suit to interview in and was off to downtown to apply for the job. After taking all of the tests, they told me they would call me if they had an opening.

After not hearing from them for a few days, I called back and they told me they had an attorney that was going to be needing a secretary if I wanted to come in for an interview. I found out when interviewing with the attorney that he was going to fire his secretary and would like to hire me. He told me in a matter of a couple of years, he had had 15 secretaries and I would be the 16th.

I had no computer training but that was okay because he said they like to do their own training. I had worked for many years and was always praised by my bosses. However, he had a way of making me feel very incompetent, but I was determined to work for him.

I started the job and went in every day with a smile on my face and acted happy even though I was scared to death. All of the secretaries felt sorry for me and would tell me how bad he was, but once again, I needed the job and was going to work for him. Even though we were supposed to work from 8 to 5, he told me I could not leave in the afternoons until he told me to leave. I would just stay and work while he and other young attorneys were in his office whooping it up and then he would come out and tell me I could go home. He chewed me out one day and made me cry because one of the attorneys in the office had called him and when I gave him the message, I had spelled the name wrong. He told me there was no excuse for that because I had a phone list with all of the names on it. I had not checked it because I was working on a rush job when the attorney called and did not have time to check a phone list.

I would even get chewed out by the bus driver because I was not standing in the right place to catch the bus. I would cry from the time I got on the bus until I fell asleep at night. I literally cried so much that I had no tears left when I needed to cry. I was now alone except for Rusty and Ralph, the dogs. But I at least was making enough money to pay the bills, help Gena out and buy bologna to eat.

Once again, God took over and after working for that attorney for 6 months, he left to go into practice on his own. I then went to work for the very nicest people in the firm, Malia Litman and Joe Banks. They were exceptionally nice to me and were constantly praising my work. From this day forward, I loved my job and had nothing but nice bosses while working with Thompson & Knight for 23 years. I was even able to work overtime at nights and on the weekends to help pay for Gena's college. Even though I did not have much left over after payday, I knew I would be able to make it. I told Gena when she was home for the summer that we would have to eat Hamburger Helper in order to make it, but that did not last. We had it one time and both got sick.

During Gena's Freshman year in college, my mother hurt her back and I had to take off a week from work and go and take care of her. When I came home from Mother's house, J.D. was gone and I did not hear from him until Gena came home for Thanksgiving and I told her that I had no idea where her Dad was. He called her after she was home to tell her he would not be back home. This was the day before Thanksgiving and I was a mess. I was having Thanksgiving lunch at my house and had not even been to the grocery store to buy the groceries. I went through the motions of going to the grocery store like a zombie and tried to be strong for Gena.

Right after Gena went back to college after Thanksgiving J.D. came back to get his clothes and some dishes and furniture. We both cried, but knew in our hearts it was the right thing for him to do because I had been hurt so many times and had had so many sleepless nights without him coming home that it was not good for my health.

I was not only heart broken, but also scared to death. Even though J.D. agreed to my keeping the house, I was also left with the house payment, insurance on the house, utilities to pay, a daughter in college and a worn out Subaru to drive.

With Christmas just around the corner and no money, I was pretty well devastated. I asked Mother if I could borrow $500 to buy Gena Christmas presents, which I eventually was able to pay back. I did everything possible to make it a good Christmas; even went out and bought a beautifully decorated tree. It was a pretty lean Christmas but we survived it.

While Gena was in college, I found out that my lifetime friend, Susie Taylor, was also in the process of getting a divorce and we hooked up. This is when the survival began. Susie had gone to Divorce Recovery at Park Cities Baptist Church and said if I would go, she would go with me. This helped us both tremendously because when you are going through a divorce, you have feelings like you have never had before, i.e., like it was all your fault and you are a complete failure. You have an overwhelming feeling of rejection because you have not only lost your best friend but also the love of your life. In this class, we learned how to deal with our feelings and how to go on with life.

We then started going out with Vanita, her neighbor who was also divorced and Betty, who worked with Vanita and was divorced. Vanita had heard about a place called Parents Without Partners where everybody that went there was divorced and we started going there to dance.

We would go and nobody would ask us to dance and we decided that maybe there was something wrong with us. We actually looked better than most of the women that went there, but finally figured out it was because they all knew each other and the women would ask the men to dance. After going there several times, we were finally asked to dance. This is where I met a very dear friend, Jim, who would sit with us and always asked me to dance. I was not divorced at the time and would not date anyone but loved to go and dance and then come home.

We started taking dance lessons at PWP and I would work all day and head home to get ready to go to dance lessons, and then we danced every Friday and Saturday night.

One Saturday Susie had heard of this place that had dance lessons; I think it was the Cadillac Bar or something like that, and she talked me into going. There was no air conditioning and it was hotter than blazes, but we had a great time. I went to a class where they taught "dirty dancing" just like the movie and my partner was about 6 foot 5. It was the most fun dance I have ever done and we laughed until we could not even dance because he would have to get almost on the floor for me to do some of the moves. After dancing all day, we then loaded up and headed to PWP. We decided on the way that we would stop at Luby's Cafeteria and go in their restroom and wash up because we were so sweaty and did not have a dry thread on us.

While running around with Susie, she invited me to go on a ski trip to Colorado with the law firm she was working for, Baron & Bud. I agreed to go but had no ski clothes, no snow boots or anything and could not afford to buy them. My friend Sherri Farmer said she had a couple of ski suits that I could borrow and even had a big duffel bag that everything would fit into, so I borrowed these. My cousin Cheryl had a pair of snow boots she would loan me, so I was in business. After packing everything, I could not even lift the bag off the luggage carrier at the airport. Finally, we made it to the ski lodge and wouldn't you know, our condo was on the second floor with very steep stairs. There were five of us staying in the Condo, so we formed a line up the stairs and sent my stuff up piece by piece until I was able to carry the bag up. Anyhow we had a good laugh out of this.

The next day we were off to get fitted for skis so we could take ski lessons. After the lessons and skiing down the bunny slope, one of the ladies' daughter that was with us wanted me to go with her the next day and ski down a mountain. I must have been crazy, but agreed. We were going up the ski lift and she kept pointing to the road we would be skiing down and I told her I don't do roads. I was beginning to get really scared and by the time we got to the top, I told her I wanted to just ride the ski lift back down. She said they did not allow this and when it came time for us to get off, I just jumped off and fell first thing. We then proceeded to the first slope we had to ski down and it was horribly steep; nothing like the bunny slope I had skied down. I knew right away I was doomed. I skied all the way down the mountain with my skis in the stopping position and at times, I would start going so fast that I would just run up the side of the mountain so I could fall. After resting for a few minutes, she would help me up and we were off again. She kept telling me what a good job I was doing and literally talked me all the way down the mountain. I kept begging her to call for a body bag to take me down, but she would just insist that I keep going. It took us all day long to ski down this mountain and my legs felt like spaghetti by the time we got to the bottom. I told everybody that I had rather drive all over Dallas in a car with no brakes than to ski down another mountain.

On this trip we also went snowboarding, which was a lot of fun, and went up into the mountain at night on a sled pulled by horses to a cabin in the woods for dinner. The scenery was absolutely beautiful and the sky was so breathtaking. It looked like you could reach up and pick a star out of the sky.

On this trip, all of the attorneys had nice clothes and snow boots and then there was me with the boots Cheryl loaned me that started coming apart and I was leaving a trail wherever I went. I made the decision to just throw them away and at least did not have that weight on the way home. Overall, the trip was wonderful and we had such a good time and many laughs.

While going to PWP, Susie met a man named Frank and started dating him, eventually marrying him. Vanita met a man named Mickey and started dating, so this left me and Betty. We continued to go every Friday and Saturday night and had so many good times together. I'm not sure I would have survived without these great friends, and dancing.

Jim came over one night for dinner and went back to the car to get something and left the front door open. This was a wonderful opportunity for Rusty to walk out the front door. We spent hours searching for him and could not find him. The next day my sister and I went to the pound and found a dog that looked like him, but this dog looked pitiful. He was wet and just about out of it. I called his name and he recognized it, so I knew it was Rusty. I paid the $25.00 to get him out of the pound and came home and bathed him and all was good. A few days later, I received several citations via Certified mail from the City of Garland. The citations were almost $500.00 for having a dog running loose, no collar, and not being registered with the City. I had no choice but to go to Court, so I took off work and went to the Municipal Court to set a Court date. When it came time to go to Court, I had to take off again and I told the Judge I did not have the money to pay the fines and asked him if I could serve time in jail instead. He said absolutely not and lowered the fines significantly.

Jim and I remained friends and dance partners for about four years. Even though he was so sweet and kind and we had so much fun together and loved each other so very much, I decided I had better sever our friendship because he had a drinking problem that I knew I could not deal with.

I then went to PWP by myself one Friday night and the only other person there that I knew was Gary Bradley. We danced and then he walked me to my car and kissed me goodnight on the parking lot. He wanted to know if he could have my phone number so he could call me. He did call and we started dating. We have now dated on and off for about 23 years.

When it came time for Gena to graduate college, I wanted to do something very special for her even though I did not have much money. We planned a luncheon for all who attended graduation. I was really dreading the graduation because I knew J.D. would be there with his girlfriend, who was soon to be his wife. I invited them to the luncheon. When I went to pay the bill, J.D. followed me and offered to pay for half of it. I did not want him to, but he insisted. After the luncheon, I walked up to him on the parking lot and hugged him and told him how much I appreciated all he had done to help get Gena through college.

Gena moved back home and lived with me until she found a job and later moved into an apartment. She lived there for quite some time and then on New Year's Eve, there was a fire in her complex and due to smoke damage, she had to move back home. She felt very lucky that she did not lose everything.

Right after Gena moved back into her apartment, she had left town with her girlfriends for a weekend on the river at Wimberley, Texas. While she was gone, I had been dancing on Friday night and due to so many prank calls I was having during the night, I decided to leave my phone off the hook and sleep in the next morning. About 8 a.m., there was a knock on my front door and when I went to the door saw Kristi, J.D.'s wife, standing there. My heart sank and sure enough, she was trying to get in touch with Gena to let her know her dad had passed away. He had a massive heart attack and died. I had no idea how to get in touch with Gena and went into her room and luckily found a Daytimer she had left here when she moved. I started calling her friends to find out if they knew where she was or even the last name of the girl she had gone with to her Grandmother's house. After spending all morning on the phone, I finally found somebody who knew the name of the Grandmother. I called and told her friend, Barbara, and got the address but told her not to tell Gena until I could get there and tell her. I called my friend Gary who I had just started seeing and asked him to ride with me and he was happy to do so. I drove to Wimberley, told Gena about her dad, loaded her up and drove back to Garland, getting back home about 2 a.m. She then had to be in Winnsboro the next morning to help Kristi make the arrangements. I spent my birthday driving Gena to Winnsboro to help make J.D.'s funeral arrangements. It was the worst birthday I have ever had. Besides all of that, I knew what kind of funeral J.D. had always said he wanted, but had to keep my mouth shut. That was very difficult for me. Even though I had peace and contentment in my life, I never had closure until J.D. passed away.

The last time I saw J.D. alive was on my 50th birthday. Gena had put a sign on my fence that said "Lordy, Lordy, Carolyn is 50. J.D. knocked on my front door and my heart sank, once again. He said he was in the neighborhood and noticed the sign on my fence and wanted to wish me a Happy Birthday. He also said my yard looked good, but my rose bushes needed trimming. I told him he was welcome to do it because I did not have any clippers. He trimmed my rose bushes, gave me his clippers and left. It was good to see him, but only opened up the wounds as my heart longed for him to at least hug me, which he did not do.

I did have a wonderful 50th Birthday with a party planned by me, which was a dancing party. All of my dancing friends attended and we had a great time. The next day, unbeknownst to me, Gena had planned a surprise party at the clubhouse of the apartments where she was living. My lifetime friends all attended this party and was I ever surprised.

My friend Dina then took me on a trip to Jamaica for my 50th birthday. Even though I had bronchitis when we went on this trip, we had a wild time, partying every night. It was an all-inclusive place and they provided a lot of entertainment. They even had a beach party one night. Dina and I and one other large, ugly guy were the only single people at this resort, even though after having a massage, he looked pretty good. All of the couples were starry eyed and all over each other. I told Dina we could probably have any man we wanted before the week was over, just joking with her. At this beach party, we played games and one game was where the guys had to go between the girls' legs, sort of like musical chairs. When this guy had to go between my legs, he said he would have to dig a tunnel to get between my legs and this made everybody laugh.

We went out on a party boat and everybody was hanging on for dear life when we started out, but coming back was a different story. We were all dancing all over the boat and not even holding on. Maybe a little alcohol involved.

The only problem we had was that Dina would put her arm around me while we were viewing the pictures that they had taken and I would have to get onto her because I didn't want people to think we were lesbians. She also wanted to make a train when we were doing the calypso around the beach and I told her she could not make a train unless there were at least three people. We laughed a lot about this.

One night I was really feeling bad and decided to see if I could get some bourbon at the bar to help with my cough. Boy did that bartender ever fix me up. It wasn't long until I was in the Kareoke bar. I had told Dina I was going to the room because I wasn't feeling too well. When she started to the room and walked past the Kareoke bar, she heard someone singing real loud and lo and behold, it was me singing Ain't That a Shame as loud as I could. She came in and we sang the night away. What a fun trip, and sure enough, we were the only couple that was even speaking by the time we left the resort.

The only other surprise party I had was for my 40th Birthday. This was held on the Saturday before I turned 40. J.D., Gena, my sister and neighbor, Jonnie Hall planned this party. Laura Jane was visiting for the weekend and she and Gena were going to Audubon Park to swim and my friend,

Barbara Hall, had asked me to go with her shopping for some sandals. We started out at SAS shoe store that was just a few blocks away from the house. She tried on every pair of sandals in the store but did not find what she was looking for. We then proceeded to Town East and shopped for hours there and she still did not find what she was looking for. I told her that I was worn out and needed to go home and fix dinner but she kept on shopping. I began to get really upset and made up my mind that I would never go shopping with her again unless we went in my car. She finally agreed to take me home, but on the way home she decided that she liked a pair of sandals that she found at SAS and if I didn't mind she wanted to go back there and get them.

When we finally pulled up in front of my house, Clara and Jerry's van was out front and it really scared me because Laura was supposed to stay all weekend and the following week with us, so I just knew something bad had happened to her while they were swimming. Barbara decided to come in with me to make sure everything was okay and when we opened the front door of my house, which I had left dirty, it was filled with clean shiny people. Needless to say, I was a hot mess and was blown away. I couldn't even speak I was so shocked. When I came to my senses, it was great fun.

So much for the birthdays, so we will go on with my life.

I was dating Gary when I stopped at the EZ Mart on the way home from work one day and Pete pulled up beside me in his pickup. It was the first time I had seen him since Dorothy had passed away. We visited for a few minutes and I asked him to come by as I was going to fix spaghetti for dinner and he could eat with me and visit. He was on his way home from the cemetery, which I think he visited every day. He accepted the invitation and came over and we ate and visited for a long time. When he started to leave, he said he needed a hug.

I did not hear from Pete again for a few days and then he started calling and we would talk on the phone for a long time. We would relive old times and have a lot of laughs. He then started coming to my house and would be here when I got home from work sitting out front waiting for me. He was very lonesome and felt safe with me. When Gary found out he was coming over, he was very unhappy and said I would have to make a choice between him and Pete. I assured him that Pete and I were only friends and that I would not refuse to be friends with him and would not tell him that he could not come over. He then reiterated that I would have to make a choice, so I told him that I would have to remain friends with Pete and if he did not want to continue dating, that was his choice. After this conversation, I did not hear from Gary for a very long time. I missed Gary a lot, but could not be given an ultimatum.

Of course Pete was happy that I had broken up with Gary and now the only thing he had to compete with was my going out dancing. Pete did not like this one bit and started being at my house daily when I got home from work so I wouldn't have the opportunity to go dancing with my girlfriends.

After a few months, on my birthday, he surprised me with an engagement ring and asked me to marry him. I was in deep shock but agreed to accept the ring. At the time I was not really ready for marriage because I knew he was way too much like J.D. and because of that, we would have many problems. However, he then wanted to start making wedding plans right away. We decided on a wedding date of August 26th and would be married at Lakeview Christian Church with the reception at my house. Of course he had not shared this with his kids, and Gena was just as shocked as I was. He did finally call and tell his boys and they were okay with our getting married because they wanted to see their dad happy again.

We had a very nice wedding and then went on an Alaskan Cruise for our honeymoon. While on our honeymoon, I realized that I had probably made a big mistake by marrying him instead of just remaining friends, but I had done it and I would make the best of it. On the honeymoon Pete was very moody; I guess he was feeling like he was doing something wrong and not being faithful to Dorothy, so I had to be very careful about what I said or did. In other words, I had to walk around on eggshells or he would become very unhappy. It was a wonderful cruise, and despite his moodiness, we had a wonderful time.

All the time we were married, it was like there were four people living together, i.e., he and I and J.D. and Dorothy. We had a lot of fun talking about old times. Also, Pete was very good to me and would do all the grocery shopping and cooking and have dinner ready when I got home from work. He wanted me to eat and just sit with him the rest of the evening. This was not easy for me because I was used to doing things all the time and was seldom still.

All the time we were married, I had a lot of stress in my life; i.e., a stressful job, my mother in an assisted living home in Garland needing attention, and adjusting to married life. Pete was very good to my Mother and saw to it that she had everything she needed. He would always go with me on the weekends and evenings to visit her and never complained, so that was a blessing. Mother and Gena loved Pete just as much as I did.

Actually, Pete did not want me out of his sight and the only place I would go alone was to work. He always insisted that he go shopping with me and did not even want me to go to Keno and definitely did not want me to go to the slumber parties with my lifetime girlfriends. I guess you would say he was very controlling and I was not too easy to control. Therefore, we had our fair share of problems. However, I did love Pete very much, but found that he was like living with J.D. again. He loved to make me feel stupid and unattractive and would call me a slut because of the years I had been going out dancing. Even his sons picked up on the way he treated me and would say something to him about it. I loved Pete very much and was happy to have him in my life but felt a lot of times that we should have just remained friends instead of getting married. I think he had just taken care of Dorothy for so many years that he felt he should be taking care of me the same way.

I was at work the day he suffered his fatal heart attack. I had a call at work that he was on his way to Presbyterian Hospital in an ambulance. My boss, Marcie Davis, rushed me to the hospital and I made it before he died, but because they were working on him trying to keep him alive, they would not let me in to see him.

The last time I saw Pete alive, he had followed me to the car that morning in his robe with nothing on under it and just as I was backing out the driveway, flashed me. He loved to embarrass me and also make me laugh. It was a wonderful memory.

I have so many wonderful memories to fall back on and am so happy to be a part of his wonderful family. After Pete died, I had he and Dorothy's dog, Gretchen, the Rottweiler. She adored Pete and I did not know how she would handle his being gone. I would come home from work and lay in the floor with her and love her. She did not climb the stairs so would sleep at the foot of the stairs waiting for me to come down. She eventually got to where she could not get around too good because of her hips and her weight. She was a great companion and it almost killed me when I had to have her put to sleep.

Because of this marriage, I now have four wonderful sons, two wonderful daughters-in-law, six grandchildren and 6 great-grandchildren, and Gena has brothers that she loves very much.

Once again, I have been blessed by being a part of this wonderful family. How could you ever regret doing something that has added so many blessings to your life.

After Gretchen, I had decided I was not going to get another dog and had adjusted to being alone without any animal except my Granddog, Lena. I made it for about six months when my friend Linda called to see if I had gotten a dog. Since I had not, she wanted to know if I would take her little Jack Russell. She said she had to get rid of her because she made her daughter Shareece nervous. This should have been my first clue not to take her. She said she was crate trained and she would give me her crate if I would take her. I agreed and she brought her over and left her.

I am telling you that I have never seen a dog with so much energy. She was bouncing off the walls. I could not even put my makeup on without throwing the ball every few seconds. When it came time to go to work and I would try to put her in the crate, she would get under the table and by the time I got under the table, she was under another table. By the time I caught her and put her in the crate, I was exhausted. I would have to rub her for at least thirty minutes when we went to bed at night to get her calmed down so we could go to sleep. Everybody that came to visit me could not believe that I had agreed to take this dog. However, she ended up being the sweetest, most loyal dog I have ever had. At the time I had to have her put to sleep, she was my everything. I was so in love with her and could not imagine life without her.

I am now in my golden years and am now back with Gary. We are best friends and have a wonderful relationship and love each other very much. The only problem we have to keep us from marrying is that we are both very stubborn. He does not want to live in Garland and I do not want to move to Winnsboro. We have a great time together and enjoy each other's company and our lives apart are good.

After working at Thompson & Knight for 23 years, I was able to retire in 2010. For my retirement, my family and I went on a trip to Hawaii and cruised the Hawaiian Islands. I guess you would say it was the best trip ever.

During the years I had worked since J.D. left, my vacations usually were staycations trying to catch up on things around the house, so this was a real treat for me.

Since retiring, I have been on many cruises, i.e., several Caribbean cruises and a cruise to the Pacific Northwest. I am enjoying having a week filled with Saturdays, even though I do have to break down and clean house and work in the yard every now and then.

After Sweetie Pie, I once again adjusted to not having a dog and said the only way I would ever have another dog is if God put one on my front porch. It was just too hard to give them up.

Gena felt I should have a dog and called me one day telling me about a dog a friend of hers was trying to find a home for. We went to see the little dog and it was instant love. His name was Calvin, which I did not really like but he met all criteria that I wanted in a dog; i.e., crate trained and house broken so I agreed to take him and brought him home. This was on a Sunday and for four days he would have nothing to do with me. I could not even touch him. On Wednesday after I brought him home, a young girl came to my front door wanting to know if she could use my phone to call the police. She said her dad was going to beat her, so she ran away from home. I took my cell phone out for her to use and sure enough, she did call 911 and told the police what was happening. They told her to stay at my house and they would be right over. I then invited her in to wait for them and she sat down at the dining room table crying and Calvin went over to her and she petted him and then he wanted in her lap. After she left with the police, he still would not have anything to do with me. I was very patient with him and did not pressure him and sure enough he is now a very loveable lap dog. You can't even sit down without him being in your lap.

Even though my life has not been perfect, I do know that I was put on this earth for a purpose and when my purpose is served, I will be taken away. My only prayer is that God will say, "Well done, my Child."

Printed in the United States
By Bookmasters